Neighborhood Government

Neighborhood

Government:
THE LOCAL FOUNDATIONS
OF POLITICAL LIFE

by Milton Kotler

THE BOBBS-MERRILL COMPANY, INC.
PUBLISHERS · INDIANAPOLIS · NEW YORK

The Bobbs-Merrill Company, Inc.
Printed in the United States of America
Library of Congress catalog card number 69-13097
ISBN 0-672-60720-4 (pbk)
ISBN 0-672-50762-5
Fifth Printing

Acknowledgments

It is first necessary to refer to the review of the material of this book, which appeared two years ago in the *Yale Law Journal* and convinced me by its affirmative remarks that this book should be published, after all. It followed that my secretaries, Shirley Kotarba and Myra Lewinter, should suffer my attempts to arrange the material so reviewed as a book. It took my editor, Robert Ockene, to convince me that what had been reviewed was not a book at all, and that I must write a book from the thoughts of those occasional papers on liberty and neighborhood self-rule.

The ultimate source of this writing is my friendship and common work with the people of the East Central Citizens Organization in Columbus, Ohio, and Pastor Leopold W. Bernhard, my mentor on the grace and sensibilities of men.

To my fellow colleagues at the Institute for Policy Studies, to whom I owe the freedom and encouragement to write this book; and, to my wife, Janet, about whom I cannot blithely say, "She suffered my labors," but rather that she helped me translate my musings into a book that may be understood by others, I dedicate this book.

M. K.

December, 1968

Contents

Introduction

THE NEIGHBORHOOD MOVEMENT

In the spring of 1968, the local board of New York's Ocean Hill-Brownsville school district barred the school doors to nineteen teachers and administrators. The police were mobilized as the central New York City Board of Education first ordered reinstatement, then withdrew its order. The mayor sent his negotiators, while the president of the teachers' union both proclaimed and denied that he would personally lead the nineteen into the building against the will of the neighborhood board. The district superintendent continued to bar their reentry, along with most of the 300 district teachers who struck in sympathy against that community decision. Those teachers remained out of the classrooms until the school year ended. In the fall of 1968 we witnessed the longest and most violent public school strike in New York's history.

What will finally happen in the struggle for local school control is hard to predict. It is, however, important to note the degree to which the simple assertion of local control over a public institution could confound the bureaucracy of the nation's largest city. We must not underestimate the power of neighborhood action against central administration, nor the essential vulnerability of a giant city's administration to local political demand. Neither should we underestimate the possibility of the use of police and military force to compensate for the political deficiencies of the cities.

We are witnessing a movement for local control in cities across the land. In the past several years, neighborhood residents have been organizing their territories for control of their institutions to serve their own, rather than outside, interests. Sometimes by peaceful transfer, sometimes as a consequence of rebellion, the public agencies and the real estate and business interests in black communities are coming into local hands. It remains to be seen how far this transfer will go and what varieties of local operations will develop. But it is a compelling fact that this activity is taking place as the neighborhood community pursues its own interests in corporate action. The movement of local control is a political movement.

In May 1968, the United Front of Roxbury, a predominantly black community, demanded independence from Boston. Mayor Kevin White of Boston dutifully rejected that claim. How the United Front will pursue separation is an open question. Its demand follows several years of building a political organization for the control of the local economy and public life, and it is not likely that the Front's efforts will cease because its demands have been rejected by the municipal government.

It is clear from the student seizure of Columbia University that the movement for local control is not limited to black neighborhoods. Large universities are facing the demands of their students and the surrounding neighborhoods for some governing authority. And if the reader should ask what student strikes have to do with neighborhood control, let him realize that students live in the university environs long enough for it to become their neighborhood. Their stake in its dominant institution, the university, is not dissimilar to that of the neighborhood families living in university-owned property and subject to such pressures as eviction. The demand for local control does not depend on how long one lives in a neighborhood, but on the place's serving one's own needs rather than outside interests. Thus, for students, a sufficient basis for a movement for local control would be if the university were primarily serving the defense department rather than educating its students. The argument that particular students are in residence for only four years does not weaken the claim for local control, since students are always there.

The white student uprisings at Columbia, Stanford, and other universities have a parallel in the wide scope of the neighborhood movement among the white community. Almost every middle-class neighborhood has by now organized its local association, and some, like Riverdale in New York, are already assessing themselves privately for extra services (private police, the purchase of a park), and are thereby building the practice of internal self-rule. Urban ethnic groups who can't afford additional services and have nothing civil to govern are busy building their own militias.

What are we to make of such assertions of local control and of the different kinds of organization and tactics? It is as if the neighborhood has sprung from its quiet niche in the metropolis to surprise us with its claim for local liberty.

The nation—and by that we mean those who think in national terms—is confused and disturbed by this eruption of local power and its hundred faces. Here it is the public school that the community wants to control, there the businesses in the neighborhood. Now it is control of police, again it is control of the welfare office or antipoverty center. What are we to make of this rising up of the people, not for national purposes or even for city control, but, simply, for neighborhood control?

To understand this new political movement, we must understand the nature of the neighborhood, so long ignored or misunderstood, and with that understanding we must examine the nature of the modern revolution of local control.

We are indeed in a revolution, but it is not the kind we were taught to expect. Our models were ambitious and of earth-shaking power. Carried by universal history, no less, they announced their coming through ideology. From this heritage of global revolution, however, we managed to whittle its force down to national revolution. Now, in view of the rebellion, we must further lower our sights to urban revolution; we must accept the neighborhood as the source of revolutionary power, and local liberty as its modest cause.

The informed metaphor of the bloody image of revolution has been implanted in our minds by teachers from Robespierre to Stalin. Revolution, we supposed, came with universal doctrine and violent death. We were not prepared for the intimate demands and mild disorder of local revolution. Had we known that liberty lies in a self-governing community, rather than in man's separation from it, we would not feel panic at today's movement for local control, and at the urban rebellions which our panic creates.

We had been taught that revolution springs from causes larger than men—from historic forces—when it springs, in fact, from matters which cause anger and fear and contempt in the basic situations of people's lives, such as their schools, jobs, welfare, health, and so on.

In short, our knowledge has been misguided in the direction of globalism. World power, not local liberty, captivated our imaginations for so long that it has distracted us from practical thought and civic emotions. For who really cares about the globe! That issue was settled when we discovered it was round.

On behalf of the abstract global imagination, we have deprived people of a decent local life. Our affluence has been siphoned into projects of no practical consequence, except the loss of felicity. By impoverishing millions for war and world adventures, we breed anger. The tensions of world power and the requirements of domination cause millions to fear; and the very brazenness of this misappropriation of wealth and misuse of rule earns the contempt of the remaining millions. But realizing these rebellious emotions requires a fine sensitivity toward the neighborhood, for it is in the neighborhood, not across the world or even in the nation, that people talk to each other and amplify their feelings until they move to recover the source of value in their lives. They move toward objects that neighbors understand and share—namely, the community and its self-rule, rather than its present neglect. And local control it must be, for the central government, with its global ambitions, cannot rule the neighborhood well because of what it despises—namely, local liberty.

In this new day it is important to realize that government must rule its domain, rather than aggrandize new territory. City government must rule its neighborhoods, rather than annex whole counties. Insistence on expansion, whether by nations or cities, requires oppressive control over their people, who may lose their rights as subjects living in a community of good will but do not entirely forget them. If this right is abused by governments that will not rule, there is no alternative to local liberty and self-rule. Thus two items today become apparent. People revolt when their civic emotions are abused. They do not need global doctrine when the image of good community is sufficient.

This book attempts to wipe the dust from the idea of neighborhood, and to explore the meaning of the neighborhood movement in its practical force and political spirit.

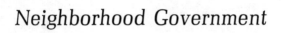

Neighborhood Government

1. *The Historical Basis of the Neighborhood*

> *If we should follow the history of these wards, we should probably find that, though reconstituted from time to time as the city expanded, they had grown out of the villages which clustered around the Acropolis when that natural stronghold had been a polis in the original sense of the word.*[1]

An understanding of the nature of the neighborhood will validate its present drive for local control as a political movement for liberty.

There are various opinions about what a neighborhood is. Baltzell argues that men and their families band together in relatively small and homogeneous groups in the

---

[1] Thomson, George, *Studies in Ancient Greek Society*, p. 364. Citadel Press, N.Y., 1965.

city in order to mitigate the loneliness and anonymity of metropolitan life.[2] The difficulty with this view is that the settlement of neighborhoods generally precedes formation of the modern city and development of metropolitan life. Thus, the Kensington neighborhood of Philadelphia was settled before the city itself. As for the homogeneity of neighborhoods, we find that to be an empty expression, except insofar as the residents of a neighborhood share a common local identity.

Park argued that neighborhoods begin as mere geographic entities and become localities with sentiments, traditions, and histories of their own.[3] But we can as easily argue the reverse, that they began as political units with self-governing charters, like the city of Lakeview, now part of Chicago, or the town of Frankford, now part of Philadelphia, and deteriorated to mere geographic expressions.

There are many other theories about the neighborhood, but they are generally propositions about its accidental features, or about properties it shares with other associations. What we require is a definition of the neighborhood and knowledge of its peculiar properties that are not shared by other units. This chapter proposes its essential definition as a political settlement of small territory and familiar association, whose absolute property is its capacity for deliberative democracy.

Germantown is a neighborhood of Philadelphia. It was

[2] Baltzell, E. Digby, *Philadelphia Gentleman*, p. 173. Free Press, N.Y., 1958.

[3] Park, Robert E., *The City*, p. 3. University of Chicago Press, Chicago, 1966.

settled by Rhinelanders in 1683 on 6,000 acres granted by William Penn to Francis Daniel Pastorius. By 1690 it was a township of sixty houses and three hundred people. Until the last decade of the eighteenth century, German was the official and vernacular language. Thus, Germantown originated as a chartered town of Quaker immigrants, founded concurrently with Philadelphia to its south. Germantown continued as a political unit until it was annexed by Philadelphia without the consent of its residents in the consolidation of 1854. After 171 years of independent growth, that neighborhood lost its political self-rule. If we turn to Kensington or other neighborhoods of Philadelphia, we can trace their settlement and political independence to a time before Philadelphia was settled. The neighborhood of Kensington originated as the town of Schackamaxon, where the first Quaker meeting in America was held in 1682 and from which Penn oversaw the planning of Philadelphia. To the south of the original limits of Philadelphia lies the present thirty-ninth ward of the city, formerly the town of Moyamensing, and previously as Wicaco, settled by Swedish farmers before Philadelphia existed. In 1854 twenty-eight cities, towns, and boroughs lost their local government and were incorporated into the city of Philadelphia.[4] The present-day neighborhoods of Philadelphia can be traced to these original political units.

Morrisania (now part of the Bronx) was settled as a township in 1788, and by 1864 it embraced the fourteen incorporated villages of Mott Haven, North New York,

---

[4] Baltzell, *op. cit.*

Port Morris, Wilton, East Morrisania, Old Morrisania, West Morrisania, Melrose, South Melrose, East Melrose, Woodstock, Claremont, Eltona, and Dove's Neck. The present-day neighborhoods of Morrisania have no local liberty, but they retain their political identification and can be traced to these former villages.[5]

Roxbury, in Massachusetts, was settled and incorporated as a town in 1630. Its population grew rapidly and diverse villages sprang up within it. Distance and political differences caused West Roxbury to separate and become a town in 1851. Roxbury continued to exist as a self-governing unit until 1868, when it was annexed by Boston. Today, the boundaries of the Roxbury United Front, which is demanding independence from Boston, coincide with the township boundaries of the Roxbury which had existed as a self-governing political unit for 238 years.

Woodside, N.J. was originally part of Bellville, which had separated from Newark and become an independent town. In turn, Woodside separated from Bellville in 1869 and was independent until 1871, when it was reannexed by Newark. A resident laments this loss of independence:

> But alas, on the fifth of April, 1871, our independence was lost forever and most of us were turned over to the tender mercies of the Newark politicians, who have ever since exercised a wonderful ingenuity in taxing us poor inhabitants to the limit and giving us as little in return as possible. . . . Does the road need paving or sewering, the cost is assessed on the abutting property, and so it is with side-

---

[5] Jenkins, Stephen, *The Story of the Bronx, 1639-1912*, p. 371. C. P. Putnam's Sons, N.Y., 1912.

walks, and even with the shade trees which the city fathers insist are good for us, and having planted them they send us a bill therefor. The Woodsider has never yet been able to ascertain what he is taxed for, unless it is to keep the politicians in good running order....[6]

Today Woodside is a neighborhood of Newark, but its name and settlement trace back to its independent polity.

Danforth, N.Y., was settled in 1874 by people who left Syracuse because they had political differences. It existed independently until 1886, when it was annexed by Syracuse.[7]

From a few examples we see how present-day neighborhoods can be traced back to original village and town settlements which were eventually annexed by the strongest political unit of the region. Thus Pittsburgh prevailed over Allegheny, and Brooklyn over Bushwick and Flatbush. Conversely, we see that our cities also began as small villages or towns which seized regional dominion—as in the case of Philadelphia, which annexed an entire county in 1854. Typically, the present central business districts of our cities represent the original boundaries of the city. Downtown Chicago is the city's present business center, and we see that center as the original boundary of the city, which was situated in a region of other towns and cities such as Hyde Park, Jefferson Park, Rogers Park, and the city of Lakeview.

Through annexation, the strongest political unit in the

---

[6] Hine, Charles G., *Woodside, The North End of Newark, New Jersey,* p. 3. N.Y. 1909.

[7] Letter from Syracuse Department of Planning.

region deprived other villages, towns, and cities of their autonomous government and controlled their territory through political party organization, which was the instrument of domination for "free" downtown. The strength of the party emanated from the power of that original city, which never lost its liberty.

How then are we to understand the political quiescence of neighborhoods after annexation? Sociologists and planners coined the current definition of neighborhood as a beneficent unit of local identity which makes city living possible. If neighborhoods originated as autonomous political units, it is consistent that after annexation the territorial identity of neighborhoods survived even if they were under firm ward control and police occupation by downtown. Yet the fact that residents continued to associate socially after the loss of self-rule did not transform the neighborhood into a social unit. It remained a political unit in which people continued to live, under domination of the central city and without local liberty.

A contemporary view of the city must take into account that the original areas of Chicago or of Philadelphia —their present-day business districts—remained the only free and independent political entities in the region, while the outlying towns, cities, and villages were annexed and subjugated to their power. Free politics exist only downtown, where financial and commercial powers decide how they will rule the neighborhoods or wards for their own benefit.

The source of political conflict in a city, then, is the competition for power among downtown interests or between downtown and the neighborhoods. Downtown has long been the only seat of political power in the city, while the neighborhoods, once political units, have not been able to exercise power since their annexation.

Several elements should be added to this characterization of the central neighborhood. Our usual allusion to downtown as a business district is misleading. For downtown remained a residential neighborhood long after it annexed the surrounding political units. Thus, long after Philadelphia's annexation of Philadelphia County, its former boundaries encompassed a residential neighborhood for rich inhabitants. Rittenhouse Square was an exclusive area until 1890, almost forty years after the consolidation,[8] and remains much, although not entirely, the same today. The special residential character of downtown persists to the present day, for the owners of major financial and commercial interests maintain residences in the central districts of Chicago, Philadelphia, New York, Boston, and many other cities. Although Chicago bankers may have family estates in Libertyville, the heads of families and owners of their interests maintain apartments or hotel suites downtown. Downtown remains a residential neighborhood for the rich who own the resources of this "free" district, which in turn rules the metropolitan region.

While the people of the neighborhoods around the central city refer to its area as "downtown," the residents of downtown refer to it as Chicago. Charles Wilson once said that what is good for General Motors is good for the country. In this same manner, the owners of downtown say that what is good for downtown is good for Chicago— meaning the 224 square miles of annexed territory.

The rhetoric advocating annexation has always been

---

[8] Baltzell, *op. cit.*

based on the efficiency of government. Yet several examples suggest other causes. Philadelphia increased its pressure for annexation in 1845, following its fear of the working-class riots of surrounding Kensington and Southwark. By 1848 the towns and villages around Philadelphia were heralding the European revolutions. Flags betokening sympathy for the revolutions were flown over the State House in Philadelphia by German, Italian, and Swedish residents of these towns. After concerted efforts by a committee of Philadelphia businessmen advocating the election of state legislators favorable to consolidation, the act effecting annexation was passed in 1854. After years of resistance, the surrounding cities, towns, boroughs, and villages lost their governments to the city, and the metropolitan region came under the single rule of small but powerful Philadelphia, then the area which is the present-day central business district.

In the case of New York City, consolidation was enacted by the New York State Legislature in 1866. It was a Republican move to break Democratic party control in New York City (then encompassing only Manhattan and Staten Island), based on working-class support, by overwhelming it with the population of villages and towns spread outside the city limits.[9]

These examples suggest that it is an error to define neighborhood as a social unit. The neighborhood is, in origin and continuity, a political unit. Although people initially choose to move into a particular neighborhood, once there, they must abide by its customs. As inde-

---

[9] Breen, Matthew P., *Thirty Years of New York Politics, Up to Date*, p. 54. N.Y., 1899. Privately published by Breen.

pendent political units, the neighborhoods were governments, and the residents made decisions about zoning, taxes, and other matters. Today, as residents of political units controlled by the power of the central city, the people are involuntarily subject to its political control. Aldermen and committeemen of the party in power make decisions affecting the neighborhood, and the residents must abide by those decisions.

The neighborhood was never a sufficient unit for friendship and social intercourse. In earlier days, the people of independent Hyde Park traveled to Chicago and back for a society that was more meaningful than that of the villages and towns. Likewise today, we know that socializing in Chicago is not limited to people's own neighborhoods, but draws upon like people throughout the city. Neighborhood is and always has been the basic unit of political life only.

The current development of neighborhood corporations to gain and exercise local control is quite consistent with the historical character of neighborhoods as political units. When neighbors organize to win control of public institutions in the neighborhood because they do not want them to be run by downtown, they are utilizing the political nature of the neighborhood. To control those institutions is to free the territory from downtown power. This independence is not something new to the neighborhood, but is a liberty which the territory is seeking to regain.

The neighborhoods today are not claiming absolute sovereignty, just as they had never been originally settled in total independence. Tracing the origin of neighborhoods, we see that they were usually settled as villages or

towns and had charters granted by provincial, proprietary
or state governments. They often had to meet certain charter requirements, principal among which was sending a representative or delegate to the councils of the chartering
government. Thus for 238 years Roxbury sent delegates
to the General Court of Massachusetts. Even after annexation by Boston, the ward of Roxbury continued to
send its delegates to the city council of Boston. The
denial of representation to neighborhoods in many cities
with at-large council election procedures is partly respon-
sible for the reassertion of neighborhood independence.

Why, after years of political subjugation, are the neighborhoods now reasserting their independence? The cause
does not differ essentially from the original cause of the
forming of a neighborhood as a political unit for self-
governing liberty. The generation and regeneration of
neighborhoods must share the same principle of political
self-rule. The years following annexation of outlying areas
by the central city saw the steady decay of the former
towns, while the inner city grew in magnificence: thus
the famed Loop of Chicago, the magnificence of midtown
Manhattan, Beacon Hill in Boston, and Rittenhouse
Square in Philadelphia. As these ruling neighborhoods
advanced, Harlem and the Bronx decayed, as did Roxbury
and Brighton in Boston. The urban province was exploited
for the economic advantage of downtown. Party politics
kept the neighborhood subservient to the central city and
its interests. The promise that brought about the acquies-
cence of the people of the impoverished neighborhoods
was that of economic opportunity.

A further cause of the advancing pace of neighborhood

power has to do with the weakening of ward control by the central city and its ruling mechanism in the political parties. Partly because their economic interests are now national and international, and no longer confined to one city, the corporations have become careless about controlling their municipal domain. In addition, the rise of a professional government bureaucracy in the cities is challenging the political party as the effective instrument of domination. Various other factors combine to weaken domination, which has given new life to the political principle of neighborhood liberty.

The outcome of the present regeneration of the political independence of neighborhoods is uncertain. The central neighborhood may take a firmer military policy toward the assertive neighborhoods, as it has in recent events. On the other hand, the cities may become more properly centralized with greater equity to all neighborhoods, under central bureaucratic control, in contrast to the former exploitation of all neighborhoods for the sake of one central neighborhood. This would require a sharp increase in the power of the administrative, rather than the political-party, machinery. Or, indeed, the political rebellion of the neighborhoods may gain them local autonomy and representation.

In whatever way the present revolution of the cities might resolve itself, the focus of our inquiry remains clear. The neighborhood, in origin and existence, remains a political unit of settlement, whether self-ruling or dominated. And neighborhood organization is the natural place for either founding new liberty or liberating local settlement from outside power.

2. *The Imperial City*

The most noticeable feature of the heart of Chicago is its size. The business of this city, covering an area of one hundred and eighty-one square miles, is substantially all done or managed in an area something less than thirty-five hundred feet square. The city has some thirty large banking establishments, nearly all of which would be embraced in a circle with a radius of nine hundred feet. Within this circle, too, would be included the principal office buildings.[1]

The modern city differs from the neighborhood in kind, not in degree. It is an urban empire ruled by a central

---

[1] Franklin Head, "The Heart of Chicago," *The New England Magazine*, new series VI (July 1892), 555-556.

neighborhood, while the other neighborhoods are political associations under its control. It is necessary to emphasize this distinction at the outset, for, as noted earlier, people generally refer to a neighborhood as a social community when in fact it is a political unit, and to a city as a political association when it is only another unit of urban society. But this does not mean the urban region which we call a city need be controlled by one neighborhood in order that there be social organization among the people of the region.

Cities in the nineteenth century abolished the governments of neighboring political units and have since controlled their territories by means of political administration for their central interests. Thus Philadelphia gained dominion over twenty-eight districts, boroughs, and townships in 1854. Before that year, there were political relationships among these neighborhoods. At present, since there is no neighborhood legal authority, municipal politics refers only to the internal politics of the one remaining political association—downtown, or Philadelphia proper —and its central political party organizations. In Pittsburgh, Detroit, and many other cities which now have city councils elected at large, neighborhood representation is not even possible. Between the ruling district and subordinate neighborhoods there is only the domination of power.

The purpose of the imperial dominion of the city is to control the neighborhoods for the sake of the economic and political interest of the central business district, which had formerly been impeded by their political independence. In the case of Philadelphia, surrounding towns imposed tolls and charges that limited the financial power of the city. Its boundaries also limited commercial development.

A petition of the town of Boston to annex Dorchester Neck (South Boston) expresses this. The current rhetoric of administrative efficiency as the guiding advantage of annexation is not present here:

> To the Selectmen of the Town of Boston:
>
> GENTLEMEN— . . . The central situation of this town, now become a county: the security, beauty and convenience of its harbor, placed at the bottom of one of the fairest and most important Bays within the dominions of the United States, conspire to raise it to the head of all the commercial towns of Massachusetts; and whilst it is fast progressing to the distinction of being the Emporium of the five Eastern States, common prudence and judicious enterprise must forever secure to it this enviable advantage.
>
> The rapid increase of her population, the various avenues now opening, the shortening the distances and improving the roads, leading from the principal inland towns and neighboring seaports; her inestimable foreign commerce, combined with an extensive coasting trade, both annually augmenting and rousing the energies of her citizens, will soon imperiously require an enlargement of the boundaries with which this metropolis is now circumscribed.[2]

The imperial purpose of the modern city functions on the basis of three principles. One is to monopolize all re-

---

[2] Simonds, Thomas C., *History of South Boston*, pp. 279-80. Boston, David Clapp, 1857.

gional political power in the original city, or downtown.
Thus we can trace the rapid elimination of any independent political identity of the annexed towns until they are
reduced to mere local units of residence or industrial areas.
The stages of political domination have generally begun
with the conversion of the annexed town into a ward with
elected aldermen and common council members. During
this stage some wards continued, as in Pittsburgh, to be
a separate school and court district. In other cases, as
in Boston, it lost these powers upon annexation and retained only representational rights. Next the old wards
were gerrymandered, and their political identity was
further diffused. When South Boston was annexed, it was
combined with the more populous South End of Boston.
The two sections together formed the twelfth ward, where
the people of South Boston and their particular interests
were scattered. At the end of the nineteenth century, a
further stage of municipal reform eliminated ward representation in favor of at-large elections and even withdrew
remaining local authority over school districts. Pittsburgh
was "reformed" in this way in 1911. At the completion of
that stage, nothing remained of the independent governments of the neighborhoods.

The second purpose of annexation was to exploit the
wealth of the region until the neighborhoods became
impoverished, while downtown became enriched. This can
be seen in the destruction of formerly independent centers
of commerce in the region, and the consolidation of financial and commercial power downtown.

The fatality to local enterprise is poignantly argued in

the petition of Dorchester Neck to the Massachusetts legislature opposing annexation by Boston in 1804:

> Should Said Neck, which may be more properly called the head of Dorchester, containing nearly six hundred acres of land, first in Quality, inviting the Citizens of all counties to its extensive shore, be annexed to Boston, already the successful rival of every Town in the Commonwealth, the remaining part of the Inhabitants of Dorchester must lose their balance in the scale of Government—and for want of proper objects to draw the Spirit of Enterprise and Industry into action, and means to regain their former station, must remain in the background of their fellow citizens, with a large number of poor to support, many Roads to maintain and new ones to make, and no Diminution of their Town charges.[3]

After many attempts, Pittsburgh annexed Allegheny's territory of 24,504 acres and its population of 140,000 in 1907. That final triumph over a strong manufacturing and commercial city caused Robert Woods to say in 1914, "The time is soon coming when all the large industries will be eliminated from the city, and Pittsburgh proper will become simply the commercial and cultural headquarters of its district."[4] It is important to note Woods' reference to downtown as the "city," or "Pittsburgh proper."

As to the impoverishment of neighborhoods which resulted from this central consolidation of financial and commercial power, we have only to recall the plea of currently

---

[3] Simonds, *op. cit.*, p. 278.
[4] *The Pittsburgh Survey, the Pittsburgh District—Civic Frontage, 1912,* p. 16. Russell Sage Foundation, N.Y.

decrepit South Boston, when it petitioned for separation
from Boston in 1845:

> Many of our inhabitants (10,020) have not only their
> houses, but their business, upon the peninsula. The
> amount of capital actually invested in manufacturing es-
> tablishments alone is estimated at nearly fifteen hundred
> thousand dollars . . . and the valuation for the current year
> is estimated by competent persons at above $5,500,000.[5]

South Boston failed in its plea, though it foresaw its
decline:

> However, the mere prosperity of a place is no test of its
> real worth. . . . South Boston has been sought as a residence
> by a very respectable class of persons, rather in spite of the
> policy which the city government has pursued with regard
> to the place, than in consequence of it.[6]

The third purpose which annexation served was to im-
pose on the subjugated political units the burden of paying
disproportionately the costs of the city administration.
The taxation study of the Pittsburgh Survey of 1912 noted
that in:

> the downtown wards where, in spite of full classification,
> the rates were hardly more than two-thirds of those as-
> sessed against small business properties along Wylie and
> Center Avenues in the old thirteenth ward; note, again,
> the rate of 8.52 mills assessed upon the large unimproved
> holdings in the southeastern part of the old twenty-second
> ward, as compared with the rate of 18.7 mills paid in the
> dense tenement house districts up the hill from the busi-

---

[5] Simonds, p. 308-9.
[6] Simonds, p. 309.

ness section of the Point. Still again, note the expensive residence quarter of northeast of Schenely Park which paid two-thirds the rate paid by small home owners in the Oakland, Bloomfield and Lawrenceville neighborhoods.[7]

In that same study, we note that the neigborhood of Beltzhoover, annexed in 1898, paid a subdistrict tax rate ninety times greater than that paid by the old third ward, which was part of the downtown.[8]

These three elements of imperial control were achieved in most eastern cities by the last decade of the nineteenth century. Since then, the escape of neighborhood populations to the suburbs has imposed a new need for expansion under the current name of metropolitan government. The purpose is the same as it was then—namely, to destroy the suburban governments and quash their independent commercial growth and political power, as well as to burden their residents with proportionately the greatest costs of central administration.

Popular opinion holds that our cities have grown. This is true in one sense, for the dominion of downtown, the original city, has increased through the destruction of surrounding cities, towns, and boroughs. Thus the area of dominion of Philadelphia was 2 square miles from 1682 to 1854. In that year the city persuaded the state legislature to obliterate neighboring political entities, and Philadelphia's dominion increased to an area of 129.714 square miles. Since then its territory has remained the same. We

---

[7] *The Pittsburgh Survey, op. cit.*, pp. 182-86.
[8] *Op. cit.*, p. 179.

can hardly speak of Philadelphia as growing in size, when
it expanded only once. This is not growth in our normal
sense of the word, but a territorial seizure.

In the case of New York City, we see growth by annexation in which the city first encompassed only Manhattan
and Staten Island, then annexed Queens and the Bronx,
until it finally gained Brooklyn in the consolidation of
1898. The important point, however, is that it is incorrect
to refer to the past development of New York City as
growth. By the time Brooklyn was annexed, that city had
itself gone through a period of great expansion through
annexation. When the cities of Brooklyn and Williamsburg
and the town of Bushwick were consolidated in 1855,
Brooklyn became the third largest city in the Union, with
a population of 200,000. Brooklyn was the fifth largest city
in the United States in 1898, when its independent government was abolished by New York State, and its territory and people given to New York. What we usually call
the growth of New York is really the growth of Brooklyn,
Flatbush, Harlem, Flushing, etc. These former cities and
towns grew independently, only to see the benefits of their
own growth reaped by New York City.

Originally, Allegheny grew through internal development and annexation of smaller towns, and was eventually
itself annexed for the benefit of Pittsburgh. Thus the dy-
namics of urban growth must be understood in a radically
different fashion from what is currently supposed. The
impetus of urban growth is a function not of the city as a
whole, but of its neighborhoods. Urban growth had its
roots in the independent political power of the neighborhoods.

In terms of financial and commercial power, urban growth involved principally the monopolization of regional financial power in the original city, or downtown. After Allegheny lost self-rule in 1907, it declined commercially, while Pittsburgh proper absorbed its commercial power. After Brooklyn was annexed in 1898, its rate of growth also declined. In the case of Germantown, its present commerce hardly matches its state of well-being and its prospects in 1854. The discomforting fact remains that, as concerns economic growth, it is only the financial and commercial power of downtown that grows.

The same principle may be applied to population growth. Statistics show New York's population increase from 1890-1900 to have been 2,096,370. This seems amazing, except that most of the increase came about with the annexation of Brooklyn, population 1,166,582. In short, its population grew at a rate far less than its increase by annexation. If we take the population growth of Pittsburgh from 1900 to 1910, we see an increase from 321,616 to 533,905. But this increased population is not Pittsburgh's increase. It represents in greatest part the annexed populations during that decade. In fact, the territory of Pittsburgh gained only 56,339 in population during that decade, for the annexation of Allegheny alone accounted for 140,000 people. Thus, in that decade of heavy immigration, Pittsburgh's population increased only 17 per cent rather than the 68 per cent which the statistics suggest. Seventeen per cent is hardly an astonishing internal population increase for a decade. It should also be noted that the population growth rates were often greater in annexed units than in annexing cities. Thus, from 1880 to 1890, the city of Brooklyn had a population increase of 27 per cent as against New York's increase of 13 per cent. Most of the growth which histories of the Progressive era attribute to cities is accounted for by annexed populations, and the principal cause of the urban problems of that period stemmed more from that fact of domination than from growth.

The imperial growth of our cities has always required their political partnership with the state legislatures and the courts. In the case of Philadelphia, it took the business community five years of effort to secure the election of enough sympathetic Pennsylvania legislators to vote the consolidation of 1854. Generally, the initiative on behalf of annexation comes from the commercial interests of the central city; the task is then to secure election of enough favorable state legislators to vote approval of the design. In the case of New York and other cities, the annexations after the Civil War were promulgated for the purpose of breaking the Democratic Party control of the city, by enlarging it to include Republican sections.[9] In the case of Pittsburgh, a predominant purpose of annexation was to have the neighboring towns and cities carry Pittsburgh's excessive railroad debt.

Party politics has also played a role in the expansion and control of urban dominion. Unfortunately, too much attention has been given to the municipal significance of party politics. It is as if the parties were the source, rather than the manifestation, of urban politics. We can see the true role of party politics in municipal government only from the perspective of the political development of the

---

[9] Breen, Matthew, *Thirty Years of New Politics*. New York, 1898. Privately published by Breen.

original downtown city, and the requirements for controlling its annexed territories.

The original settlement of our major cities was usually democratic. There were town meetings in New York, Boston, and Pittsburgh. In New England, the informal democracy of the village settlements was institutionalized in town meeting government. Thus we find that before 1822, the areas of Boston, Dorchester, Roxbury, Charleston, and other towns comprised a region of democracies.

In these town democracies there were factions, but not organized political parties. The principal division in the assembly, as we see in the history of Quincy, was along class lines, and these came to coincide with the division between natives and immigrants. It is precisely on this class division that Quincy abolished her direct democracy and instituted the aristocratic form of municipal government, based on elected representatives. Boston had done this earlier, in 1822, with its aristocracy reflected in the first mayors, John Phillips and Josiah Quincy.

The aristocratic form of municipal government which replaced democracy provided for the division of the city into wards and for the election of councilmen and aldermen from these wards. Under most of the city charters, the mayor was not popularly elected but was chosen from among the aldermen. This was the case in New York, Philadelphia, Chicago, Columbus, and Pittsburgh. In the case of Philadelphia, already a city in 1701, the mayor was not popularly elected until 1839.

Under aristocratic city charters, the number of elected councilmen was larger in proportion to population than it is in most cities today. This was particularly true in Boston, with a population of 44,000, where each of the twelve wards elected four councilmen. After Columbus ratified its charter of 1834, four aldermen were elected from each of five wards. In Columbus, for a few years after 1834 there was a council member for every hundred population. Thus, under aristocratic rule, there was a much higher ratio of councilmen to population than there is today.

Under the aristocratic charters of municipal government, political party organizations began to develop. The parties reflected the basic rivalries within the aristocracy. Before the American Revolution there were Tories and Rebels. Among the Founding Fathers, we see an aristocratic social basis among the Rebels very similar to the Tories who evacuated New York and Boston. After the United States gained independence, the aristocratic social basis was perpetuated in the division between the Federalists and the Republicans. The last stage of aristocratic rivalry was the division between the Whigs and the Democrats. The Civil War signaled the end of aristocratic politics. For most cities, the end of the Civil War and Reconstruction were the harbingers of the local change of city governments into oligarchies, or plutocracies, as they were commonly called. With this degeneration, annexation proceeded boldly. Thus New York began consolidating in 1868; Boston annexed Dorchester, Charleston, and Roxbury in that same decade. During this period the financial centers, in collusion with the state legislatures, commenced their full-scale regional exploitation.

The decline of municipal aristocracy into oligarchy brought with it a sharp reduction of the proportion between councilmen and population. In Columbus, for instance, the ratio of councilmen to population was .01 when it was a borough, in 1816. The ratio declined to .001

by 1840, when it was a city. By 1872, it had declined even further, to .0005. Today, it should be noted, Columbus has only nine councilmen, representing a population of approximately 500,000.[10]

During the period when aristocracy was declining into oligarchy, single party domination was the principal instrument for control and exploitation of annexed territories. When the oligarchies were finally consolidated and had succeeded in eliminating the last traces of aristocratic power (the Progressive movement reflected this in part), the municipal reform tactic of nonpartisan and at-large elections of city council members completed the oligarchic form of city government. Most cities today have this form —for instance, Boston, Detroit, Pittsburgh, San Francisco, and Columbus.

Along with oligarchic consolidation has come bureaucracy, which has largely replaced political parties in their function of territorial control of neighborhoods. Some cities retain strong political party control of the dominion, under a powerful mayor, to serve this administrative function for the oligarchy. Chicago is a case in point. In other cities, the strong mayor uses the bureaucracy for this purpose.

The present movement on behalf of neighborhood control signifies the decline of the city oligarchies. One cause of decline is the inadequacy of the city's constitutional authority. State government continually diminishes the administrative flexibility required for territorial control. New York is an excellent case in point. A further cause of

---

[10] Studer, Jacob H., *Columbus, Ohio: Its History, Resources and Progress*. Published by the author, Columbus, 1873.

decline is that an inadequate financial base is left in the urban region which must still dominate immense territories. For example, in 1968, New York's budget for expenditures exceeded its income by a billion dollars. An additional cause of decline is the professionalization of municipal officials. They have lost the old popular base of party politics and are inadequate agents of rule.

At this juncture of declining oligarchy in the cities and new neighborhood action, we will see political change in several directions. Because wealth is now wedded to the national corporate structure, continued domination of neighborhoods by downtown will require other means of control, such as increased reliance on police. Such an occurrence is likely to result in a dictatorial form of government in the cities.

There are, however, two possible *civil* reconstitutions of the city. The cities may become decentralized and territorial liberties may be vested in the neighborhoods, which will federate in a common city government. This would require a decentralization of downtown wealth, for as long as downtown remains the center of finance and commerce, local liberties are not secure.

Another direction possible is the bureaucratization of municipal government, under national control. In this way federal funding and administration could apply resources more equitably to different neighborhoods, in the absence of local control. But this would, in effect, require the abolition of municipal autonomy.

Only by understanding the American city as it is today —a floundering empire, no longer in control of the neighborhoods it has annexed—can we see the force of neighborhood power in its claim for liberty.

3. Theories of Neighborhood Organization

From our inquiry into the nature of the neighborhood and the city, we can see that the purpose of neighborhood action today is to regain self-rule and representation in municipal government. This is the goal of the present struggle between localities and metropolitan empires, and it requires that we determine the most effective organization of the neighborhood for this struggle.

Our purpose in this survey is to point out what is valuable and dismiss what is erroneous, for we hope to propose the most practical theory of neighborhood organization to secure local liberty.

One theory of local organization prominent in recent years is that advocated by Saul Alinsky and currently employed in a number of cities through his Industrial Areas Foundation—such as The Woodlawn Organization in Chicago (TWO), FIGHT in Rochester, and BUILD in Buffalo. Alinsky's goal is to develop sufficient mass power to force municipal government and established power to change their oppressive domination of the poor. According to this theory, the key to activating mass power is a wide territorial organization uniting existing local organizations and acting on issues of local grievance with achievable goals. Alinsky requires an alliance of existing neighborhood organizations before agreeing to enter upon development of a project. Only then does the professional organizer enter—and as a veritable general. For this theory is essentially military, always requiring a consolidated local political base for mass power demonstrations. By this strategy, negotiation is the political extension of warfare.

The difficulty with this theory is that it relies for effect on the capacity of neighborhoods for militant disruptive power. To base self-rule on such power is to ignore the effective cause of present local domination, which is the police and military power of downtown. Unlike small independent countries, neighborhoods cannot presume to succeed in military action against a central power since they are not defending any present liberty. Barring a general uprising of an entire metropolitan population, no single neighborhood or area can defeat the central power of downtown, enforced by police. And it is not Alinsky's expressed object to cause general revolution.

Thus, his principal error is to suppose a neighborhood can succeed militarily where it has failed politically. Those which are still independent, like Evanston, Ill., or St. Bernard, an enclave in Cincinnati, have retained their autonomy because of the effectiveness of their government and the loyalty of their citizens, whose vote has consistently opposed annexation attempts. Self-rule is not the assertion of military power, but the good rule of authority, gaining the cohesiveness and commitment of localities to their independence.

This is not to say that war or threat of it against the central power is not a proper tactic in the struggle for neighborhood self-rule; but it should be used only in defense of achieved local authority, not as an offensive policy to acquire authority. The neighborhood organization must gain local authority by political means, but it must be prepared to defend gains in jurisdiction by the threat of war to any who would endeavor to deny these gains.

It is precisely with respect to the importance of military strategy in neighborhood organization that Alinsky has made a leading contribution. We must, however, adapt his strategies to defensive purposes. For example, because Alinsky emphasizes offense, he chooses extensive territories and populations for mass organization. Yet the exigencies of large territories and populations require an immediate alliance of existing organizations in the territory in order to stabilize the political base of the community for mass action. Alinsky believes there is neither time nor necessity to develop a unitary political organization. Consequently, the achievement of political authority by the community as a whole is impeded, for each allied organization will claim power and decry any gains to the allied organizations. The organizers then must choose between forsaking this organization entirely and causing envy among those allies who do not secure the authority. Alliance for military offense favors the former course, and little authority for local self-rule can develop. On the other hand, if we convert military strategy to defensive purposes, then small neighborhoods and unitary organization can exist, and effective political gains will be possible.

To date, the principal result of The Woodlawn Organization in Chicago is the rise of a military cadre—the Blackstone Rangers. Yet the organization, after having gained many tactical victories, still has no legitimate political jurisdiction, while the city government is continually arresting and jailing members of the Rangers. This demonstrates Alinsky's failure to recognize that although neighborhoods are natural political units—and thus are able to gain political authority by political means—cities are dominated by downtown power enforced by police control, and they have military force superior to any of their constituent areas.

In the past several years, chapters of the Students for a Democratic Society (SDS) have begun a number of local projects in both the white and the Negro communities of Chicago, Cleveland, Newark, and Oakland. Their foremost theoretician of community action is Tom Hayden, who led their principal effort in the formation of the Newark Community Union Council. That effort has been abandoned, but during the course of its activity and since then, Hayden and others in SDS have been constructing a more complete theory of community organization.

This theory rests mainly on the view that national revolution is required in American society if the poor are to gain political and economic equality. They claim that existing social structures cannot be pressured by groups using the tactics of Alinsky, for they are too locally oriented to bring about the changes necessary for social equality. Inherent resistance to change is not simply the opposition of established local power, but is owing rather to oppression by the interconnected structures of the national economy and its power. Thus, change essentially presupposes a national attack; local revolution is not sufficient. Accordingly, SDS puts more emphasis on organizing around national issues such as the federal antipoverty program, welfare legislation, opposition to the war in Vietnam, draft resistance, and so on. Local inequity must be traced to the national structure of power and to national issues.

In this theory, community organization is a revolutionary notion which may topple national structures of power, and self-rule liberates citizens to change national institutions and participate in national power. In this sense, community action is the organization of people to participate effectively in the national struggle. Its value is essentially strategic; it is thought that this sort of activity will develop consciousness and knowledge of national power. For SDS, self-rule entails not local self-sufficiency or neighborhood authority, but neighborhood organization as an essential unit for mobilizing consciousness and action for national revolution.

The principal value of the SDS theory of community organization is its program for advancing popular revolutionary consciousness. As they organize, people in the community learn about the structures of national power and what they are up against. They see, by comparison among the communities of various cities that have SDS local projects, common conditions of inequality, and they formulate a view of the national elements of control common to all. Significant success in bringing white and black poor, as well as students and community people, together has been made through these projects. And this interaction brings forth a revolutionary cadre for national strategy. The community then is also the action unit of this emerging revolutionary class. Further, the emphasis on knowledge of the national power structure is a strong basis for selecting local-confrontation issues. Recently, in the student revolt at Columbia University, the University's connection with the Institute for Defense Analysis was a major issue.

The principal difficulty of this approach with respect to self-rule is its stress on national power, which leads to a theoretical understanding of power instead of practical knowledge of its application. In this scheme, if self-rule were achieved, a community would not be able to exercise power but rather to support a national leadership group because of its political theories. One can envision an analogy with the present-day situation of the Soviet Union, now that the soviets have met their demise and a national ideology has triumphed. For that matter, the very emphasis on national power structures denies independent local capabilities, and we can only conclude that the significance of self-rule in this theory is to encourage local understanding of ideology and local support of national revolutionary groups.

Although a national corporate power structure exists, that group occupies itself primarily with questions of war and peace, imports and exports, and, to some extent, national defense. The problem is that poor neighborhoods, on the other hand, are interested principally in matters of economic legislation, and state and local governments have ample capacity to deal with these. Such matters were the historic concerns of the towns when they were the principal taxing and legislative units of government; foreign policy and imports and exports, on the other hand, were regulated by larger units of government. Municipal and state governments are more appropriate targets for those seeking neighborhood self-rule than is the national corporate power structure.

The neighborhood unit has no natural foundation for participating in national power. In fact, local authority has always been—and always must be—completely opposed to central power, which would invariably claim its liberties and attack its political basis for self-rule. The urban neighborhood, still for the most part dominated by downtown, is the least favorable base for securing national power. If consciousness of national power is to be achieved, it has been exemplified in a situation involving foreign war or foreign trade. For all the power national corporations and the military-corporate complex are gaining today, the United States remains an empire of city dominions, not yet penetrated by the central administration of the nation.

Another approach to community organization is offered by Black Nationalism, the idea espoused by Malcolm X early in his career as a Black Muslin and now a doctrine theoretically developed by Robert S. Browne, an economist on the faculty of Fairleigh Dickinson University. It is a separatist doctrine that rejects any interest in the reorganization of national power and seeks only to achieve an autonomous black territory in the United States. Clearly, this view deals with self-rule, but entirely in terms of a separate black sovereign nation. It thus subscribes to the

modern principle of political self-sufficiency through nationalism. The object of this kind of black militance is to
gain a territory of black autonomy, rather than to bargain
for local interests.

Claiming that racism is the fundamental principle of
oppression, black nationalists believe that no American
revolution which can solve the black man's problems will
occur. Hence, the only solution is a separate nation. Their
method of local organization is to deepen and enlarge
racial identity and difference and to increase the united
confidence of the race for the militant struggle for national
autonomy.

The difficulty with this approach with respect to community organization is somewhat similar to the problems
raised by the SDS approach—namely, confusion in terms
of territory and ideology. This theory assumes not only
that liberation comes solely through nationalism, but also
that a racial group is capable of nationalism in this country.
Rather than organizing the self-governing potential of
black neighborhoods, it offers only racial education and
recruitment to localities. Not content with the existence
of many small black territories, it seeks one large one, a
nation. The theory fails on the false assumption that
whites have gained self-rule because of white nationalism,
when in fact, whites do not have self-rule any more than
blacks do.

Liberal government officials are also accommodating
the movement for community power with their own inter-
pretation of its force and conceptualization of its form.
Their own theory is that what the neighborhoods demand
can be achieved by placing "little city halls" throughout
the city. Mayor John V. Lindsay of New York is the most

forceful advocate of such programs, and many social scientists and professional administrators are developing various operational plans in terms of public administration. This might be called the "human resources" approach to community organization.

There are different intentions in the advocacy of little city halls. At one level it is supposed that community power can achieve its demands if public administration is decentralized in the neighborhoods. The closer contact between the neighborhood and city administration would ensure a better delivery of the services that people need. But this is a superficial view, since no decentralization of an administration which is based on a government that aims to rule the neighborhoods for the interests of downtown will ever have the resources or disposition to deliver public services to any equitable and just degree. Hence, little city halls, under the present oligarchic rule of our cities, will only turn into improved police bastions in the neighborhoods.

There is also a better intention in this advocacy, which is grounded in the realization by thoughtful liberals that municipal government can no longer continue to exploit the neighborhoods for downtown power. Political power must move from the wealthy to the new class of professional bureaucrats. Only on this basis of independent bureaucratic power can administration ever become just, and this would include such devices as advocacy planning, ombudsmen, sub-professionals and various methods of involving the community in the decisions of professional administration. Under this view, little city halls will not only serve to build the political power of the new managerial class in public administration against downtown power, but also be local terminals of planning and just city service.

The basic difficulty of this better intention is that it misunderstands the present neighborhood demand for self-rule on two counts. First, while it is conceivable that the new class of administrators could run a good government were they to triumph over the present oligarchic power of downtown, there is no reason for the neighborhoods either to assume their triumph or to trust their goodness, so as to cease their independent action for local power. Secondly, it is a mistake to think that the political object of the present movement of neighborhood power is better services, for men primarily desire the liberty of local rule and democratic decision. On this score, the mere promise of political influence to the neighborhoods in the planning process and administration is no substitute for empowering them to actually implement local decisions.

There is another theory of community organization gaining wide interest, principally through its demonstration model in the Bedford-Stuyvesant Community Corporation in New York City, initiated by the late Senator Robert Kennedy. Under this approach, community power means economic power, and self-rule means a dollar in your pocket. Of course that project does contain elements of democratic decision and local control of services, but its primary emphasis lies in building economic power in the poor community as the basis of any future political power.

The effort aims to enlist established wealth to invest capital in the poor communities, as a basis for local employment and income. What is envisioned is the development of a "mix" of black capitalism and community ownership.

The difficulties of this plan are numerous, for it appeals to downtown interest to veritably reverse its economic policy toward the neighborhoods when there is no inclination to do so. Whatever capital that may flow into the poor communities will remain tied to downtown, rather than become an independent resource of the community. As for its contemplated element of community ownership, there is little likelihood that outside capital would wish to promote a wealth that was independent of its control.

At a more basic level this approach misunderstands the economic object of community control. That object is not to create a few black millionaires, or to make the individually poor somehow individually middle class. Instead, the object of economic power in the local movement today is that the neighborhood achieve an economy of its own to yield enough wealth to preserve its local political liberty. And no amount of outside capital, tying the neighborhood to downtown, would result in a politically independent economy for the neighborhoods.

4. *The Neighborhood Corporation*

Our review of different theories of community organization pointed to certain strengths and defects in their principles of achieving local power for self-rule. But by combining their appropriate elements and rejecting their defects, we can arrive at a practical method of local organization. That method must be directed to a purpose that is natural to men, like liberty; the physical area must be suitable for organizing self-rule; its means must accord with the actual capacities of local power; and its organizational form must serve the purpose of local liberty. We must examine each of these standards for practical organization.

Because the neighborhood originates as a political unit and declines as its local liberties are destroyed, the object of local power can be nothing less than re-creating neighborhood government which has political autonomy and representation in larger units. Some of the theorists discussed in Chapter 3 would disagree with this purpose. They see the city as the smallest unit of government and are content to organize neighborhood power to provide continuous pressure for benefits from city government. At the other extreme, some argue for separatism, and this assumes that the neighborhood is capable of total sovereignty. But the middle course of antonomy and representation along with other neighborhoods in a common city body is most practical. We have discussed the historical basis for this middle course, and it remains to comment on its intrinsic characteristics.

Men do not have the patience for the constant militancy which pressure upon the city would require. Nor are they inclined to the terrorism which separatism demands. They prefer the liberties of a recognized civil government, which can be achieved politically, to the constant mobilization of power in an area that is not a political unit.

There is also disagreement on the physical area to be organized for local power. Some theories favor large areas for organization—for instance, the Bedford-Stuyvesant Community Corporation area has a population of 300,000. Others think in terms of a black nation and seek a whole state for their race. Some theories favor a small, specific object in the neighborhood as the unit for organizing control—for instance, a school or a welfare office. Nevertheless, the best practical unit for organization lies in the middle, between large areas and single properties. It is the total territory of the neighborhood. This is because the object of local self-rule can be more nearly achieved in the neighborhood territory than in large urban areas or single institutions within a neighborhood. How can the independent civil government of a school be established, under the final control of its board, self-chosen or elected, unless a neighborhood government binds the school to the local residents? If it were not under the authority of the neighborhood government, such a single popularly controlled school would still be, in effect, a private school, and the children would tend to go to another public school in the neighborhood. Further, where would such a private school get its resources, if not from the neighborhood or city, neither of which has sufficient resources for its own school jurisdiction?

At the other extreme, one cannot organize a territory containing one-half million people like Harlem for civil government without first organizing the neighborhoods within it. This is because people already associate in neighborhoods, and before they join large area governments, they are more inclined to win independence for their own existing local associations. One cannot ask them to abandon the realization of their neighborhood associations in self-government for the sake of authority in a large area with which they feel as little in common as with the entire city. Hence the most practical unit for the struggle for local self-rule is the neighborhood community.

If the purposes of neighborhood organization are government and representation, and the physical area for its organization is the historic neighborhood, the efficient means for gaining local authority for the neighborhood will be by gaining political transfer from existing units of government. This approach lies between the extremes of militant seizures of institutions on the one hand and nonviolent boycotts and abandonment of present public institutions and authorities on the other. Both of these are impractical. Still other approaches fail as efficient means of achieving neighborhood government—for instance, claiming business control by destroying stores instead of claiming government powers for transfer to the neighborhood.

Attempted seizure causes the city government to send the police against the community. This tactic of seizure may be revolutionary in its aim of arousing people to agitate against the current city or national government, but there is no assurance that after a revolution there will be local control. Since local liberty is our object—whether before or after a revolution—it is of greatest importance that the neighborhood gain practical control of the school so that it can defend that control under any change of government.

At the other extreme, nonviolent boycott of schools and abandonment of public institutions in favor of parallel self-help endeavors do not build neighborhood self-rule. The municipal or state government is pleased at boycotts, for they give them time and opportunity to change personnel and methods under emergency conditions for more effective territorial control, and this under the name of improved service.

The efficient means of building neighborhood public authority and civil government lies in following the middle course, in a political strategy of transferring existing public authority and institutions to the control of the neighborhood. This involves organizing to press claims for transfer and local authority and holding flexible the range of tactics for negotiating political transfer.

The best practical organization for the political strategy of securing the transfer of public authority to the neighborhood is the legal incorporation of the local territory and the writing of a formal constitution of internal rule. SDS

favors narrow, disciplined party initiative in local organizing, rather than neighborhood membership and decision.
It prefers tough and hardened party leadership for maximum flexibility in behalf of revolutionary organization.
The difficulty with this extreme is that there is no total
legal territorial organization to receive and govern any
transferred authority. Thus, for example, it is hard to
imagine a city transferring school authority to a political
organization like SNCC or SDS. Even if the city should
do so, the neighborhood residents would object, and the
city would easily be able to regain the authority. Further,
the neighborhood unit is too small and familiarly associated to be governed by a party cadre. Such a cadre
would force indigenous leadership to take a stance of
opposition.

At the other extreme, there is support for informal mass
organizing and decision, which is promoted as "participatory" democracy. It opposes any formal organization of the
neighborhood into a corporate body with liabilities and
internal regulations of rule. It is complained that such
formality stifles expression and is intimidating to the
people. Mass meetings without control over objectives and
strategies are preferred to the binding decision of constituted neighborhood authority.

This argument has romantic appeal, but its strategic
difficulty is that it does not provide a legally constituted
entity to receive transferred public powers and institutions and to govern to the satisfaction of the residents.
Finally, it is an error to suppose informal political organizing is an improvement upon the existing informality of
neighborhood association. The neighborhoods are already
informally associated for social purposes, and quite ready

to be formally constituted for political purposes. Organizers will find that whereas informal mass organizing for political purposes threatens existing neighborhood leadership, formal organization for the political objectives of neighborhood government does not. It attracts local leadership forces, because the political objective of neighborhood government does not threaten existing social leadership.

The best form of neighborhood organization is the corporate organization of a neighborhood territory, chartered by the state and legally constituted for governing public authorities in the neighborhood. We call this form of organization the neighborhood corporation.

One existing neighborhood reflects this method of corporation: the East Central Citizens Organization (ECCO) in Columbus, Ohio. Four years old, ECCO is the oldest of some seventy neighborhood corporations around the country.

The neighborhood of ECCO covers approximately one square mile, with 6,500 residents. It is an area close to the central business district of the city.

Except for a small number of white residents from Appalachia, the people of ECCO are predominantly black. It is a poor community, with an unemployment rate of approximately 25 per cent before ECCO began, compared with a city-wide unemployment level of 2 per cent. Even presently it is estimated that 25 per cent of the residents are on welfare. By all statistical criteria, it is what we now call a poverty area.

ECCO originated early in 1965, when a neighborhood

church—the First English Lutheran Church—whose congregation of neighborhood residents had, for the most part, moved to the suburbs, agreed to transfer its settlement house to neighborhood control. This involved a six-year-old agency, which offered a great number of social, educational, and personal services, from a nursery school for retarded children to day care, tutoring, dances, psychological guidance, clubs for young and old, emergency welfare services, and other programs heavily used in the community. Its last annual budget under church sponsorship was $25,000.

Many neighborhood people who had been involved in the settlement on a voluntary and paid basis agreed to organize the neighborhood into a legal corporation of its residents to receive the transferred agency, gain funding for its operation, and independently administer its services through the governing constitution of the corporation.

While the local leadership continued to bring people into the organizing effort and to develop the charter and bylaws of the ECCO corporation, application was made to the federal Office of Economic Opportunity to fund the administrative structure of ECCO for a period of two years. During that time it was to develop a variety of programs for funding from other government agencies and private sources.

A grant of $180,000 was made to ECCO, and the church agency was transferred to the tax-exempt corporation in January 1966. For the next three months, organizing continued under the authority of an interim council, composed of neighborhood people and former members of the old church board, until March, when the neighborhood met in a general assembly and then elected the first official Executive Council of twenty-one. Thereafter, an executive staff was hired by the Council and its committees. At the election assembly, the authority of the settlement was completely separated from that of the church and vested in ECCO. In its first year, ECCO continued to house its administration in the parish hall. Today, while it rents the parish center from the church, it has its own offices in its own neighborhood building.

The formal legal organization of ECCO is set forth in a democratic constitution. Under the bylaws, as recently amended, any resident at least sixteen years old who lives within the boundaries of the corporate territory can sign the roster and become a member. The fundamental authority of the corporation is derived from its membership, which meets in assembly to elect the council members and chairman, and to transact legislative business over the laws, programs, and budget of ECCO. Its assemblies require a quorum of 10 per cent of the members; they have been legally convened nine times in the past three years. The Executive Council now has thirty members, elected both from the four neighborhood clubs (which existed before ECCO, and were re-formed to comprise four ECCO districts) and at large in an annual assembly. Voting membership on executive committees is open to any member of ECCO, appointed by the chairman. The council has executive authority, and legislative power is vested in the assembly.

The current annual budget of ECCO is approximately $202,947, consisting mainly of a grant from the U.S. Office of Economic Opportunity. A major program is the Youth Civic Center of ECCO, offering many youth activities in delinquency prevention, education, recreation, and job placement, and training in typing, shorthand, and crafts such as upholstering. The youth programs are governed by a youth committee of ECCO which has independence in the programming, management, and budgeting of their center. Although the council has executive authority, it has avoided interference with the youth committee. This Youth Center continues, even though its supporting grant from the now defunct U.S. Office of Juvenile Delinquency has been terminated. Many other programs are now offered in ECCO, and the organization has a large full- and part-time staff. The programs of ECCO include educational projects, such as tutoring, nurseries for retarded children, day care, adult education, and community drives for greater local control of administration and management of the local public school in the ECCO territory. In the area of housing, ECCO has a co-operative code-enforcement program with the city government, and is purchasing houses for rehabilitation and leasing to the Metropolitan Housing Agency. In employment, it successfully demonstrated a new plan for operating the state employment service office locally. It is also employing residents in a new sewing center, which is already marketing products. In the field of health, it operates a program with the Public Health Service, and has developed a plan for its own twenty-four hour Health Clinic, emphasizing night service to meet the needs of residents who work during the day. ECCO also operates a veterinary clinic. In the field of economic development, the organization has a credit union and has scheduled the opening of a supermarket. It also works closely with the federal Small Business Administration to finance local enterprise. It has an emergency welfare service and many other social service programs. Many recreational activities are offered.

This range of programs has been legislated by ECCO. Some are funded and in operation; others have been decided on but await the appropriation of funds. But this list by no means exhausts the subjects of legislative decision in ECCO, or in any neighborhood corporation.

ECCO's existence has been marked by struggle and by political development in both extra-community relations and internal government. The organization is often strongly opposed by both the Columbus Community Action Agency and the Model Cities Agency, which want to control federal antipoverty programs in the ECCO neighborhood. ECCO engages daily in political action against obstructive tactics of the city administration, and it has experienced clear-cut victories and defeats. A history of ECCO is being written, and it will illuminate the trials of the relationship with the city which challenge the object of local self-rule. But it is enough to say here that ECCO grows stronger and continues to thrive.

Within the ECCO area, the politics of democratic constitution over the past few years has enabled the residents to function as deliberative citizens. For the first time, the residents legally decide certain matters of community life. They are steadily practicing the art of political decision-making and living with and learning from the consequences of their decisions. There are factions and rhetoric in ECCO, as in any democratic polity, and new leadership is always generated by the political expression of new problems.

The continuing strategy of ECCO is to develop new, independent programs and to reach agreement with the city for territorial jurisdiction over these public activities. Thus, it succeeded in becoming the exclusive antipoverty authority in its territory. Furthermore, it has *de facto* territorial jurisdiction for youth programs. ECCO has also jurisdiction over the neighborhood public library, appointing the librarian and selecting books, while the city carries its cost. Gradually new jurisdictions are developing, and ECCO looks toward the time when it will consolidate enough power to achieve public political corporation. Then the neighborhood government will become a political entity of the municipal government.

As far as the present political character of the community is concerned, one might say that having deliberative authority has liberated the political spirit of the residents for internal government and external struggle against the city on such issues as police conduct, administration of public schools, jobs, welfare, and many other issues of public interest. ECCO residents are now orators and officials, and practical political wisdom is developing in a community where earlier the only expressions were frustration and escape. The men, women, and youth of ECCO are prepared to gain political control of their neighborhood.

We note that although the achievements of ECCO are not spectacular, they are growing and substantial in terms of the capacities of a community constantly opposed by outside forces. The mark of practical organization is not the transformation of a poor community into a paradise overnight, if ever. It is the liberation of practical political deliberation. It is success in defeating outside opposition and providing as adequately as possible for the material and social improvement of the community. Practical organization is tested by gauging how much liberty and prosperity have been achieved. In measuring, we must bear in mind that although the community is under attack, the greatest emphasis has been placed on deliberation and local control. In this respect, ECCO moves closer to the establishment of self-rule than other models of neighborhood organization, and has achieved more local liberty and representation of its neighborhood in the city. New neighborhood corporations in St. Louis, Philadelphia, New York, Louisville, New Orleans, and elsewhere have been modeled on the principles of ECCO.

5. *The Political Issues of Neighborhood Corporation*

We must understand that the programs appropriate to neighborhood corporations fall into the larger perspective of achieving and maintaining local self-rule. In meeting an internal problem, the programs aim to increase the local liberty of the neighborhood community. This does not mean that the corporation will leave untouched means to improve the prosperity of its neighborhood, or to solve conditions of unemployment and inadequate education. It does mean that these practical solutions have the essential aim of building the political strength and autonomy of the neighborhood, rather than the aim of solving problems as defined by outside power—and possibly of benefit to it.

In concrete terms, then, the neighborhood corporation will develop programs for the same reason any government does—namely, to build the political strength and welfare of its territory, be it a nation, city, or neighbor-

51

hood. But this is where the conflict between federal or municipal programs and neighborhood programs arises, for the political strength of the neighborhood decreases the authority of the central power. The over-all advantage of such a decrease in central power is that greater peace and harmony in the city will come about.

Because the neighborhood corporation exists to become the government of its own locality, its decisions will cover the same areas as those of any government—namely, finance, imports and exports, war and peace, territorial defense, and laws.

FINANCE

The problem of ways and means is basic to the political program of the neighborhood. In concrete terms, the question is one of how the corporation can get continuing funds for its operation. There are three sources of money: taxation, foundation grants and private gifts, and sales. For an organization with political authority—be it a neighborhood corporation or a government—taxation is the most lucrative source. Monies can be raised either by direct taxation, possible when the neighborhood corporation gains the taxing authority of a political unit, or by tax transfers from units of government, possible even when the corporation remains a private organization. If direct taxation is not feasible, the neighborhood can levy assessments; its problem then is to present convincing inducements to pay. Yet it is a defective means of funding, both because of the method's voluntary nature and because resources, particularly in poor neighborhoods, are insufficient and already taxed by government.

The major problem in taxation is to find a formula to fund both programs and organizational overhead. In this connection, the three principal categories are the neighborhood share of taxes collected by higher levels of authority, the transfer of authority to levy specific taxes from higher levels to the neighborhood—for instance, the cigarette tax—and neighborhood authority to initiate and collect new taxes.

Gifts of operating funds can also be made to the corporation, either privately or as public subsidies, and these could be an important source of funding. Philanthropic organizations can choose to support the political institution of local liberty as they have the social institution of medicine, and government can realize the political wisdom of gaining local loyalty through subsidies. By formulating an investment policy, the interest accrued on gifts and endowments can underwrite a substantial part of the costs of neighborhood corporation.

A third source of funding the general administration of neighborhoods can be the sale of goods and services. Neighborhood corporations are already contracting with federal, state, and municipal governments to perform social services in their territories for specific periods. Funding through sale of services is consistent with the move toward administrative decentralization.

IMPORTS AND EXPORTS

A vital function of any government, neighborhood or national, is the promotion of the domestic economy through trade. This is a crucial subject for poor neighborhoods, because they have no territorial economy. They produce nothing for outside sale and require everything to be supplied from outside. This is neither export nor import, but rather a colonial market. Everything sold inside the community is owned outside. Everything earned outside flows to outside ownership. To deal with this problem common to poor neighborhoods, the neighborhood corporation must begin to build an economy by attracting capital from outside sources. It must then develop an economic policy of productive investment in the territory, and it must exact a commitment that money earned there will stay there. Once production and trade have been established, outside capital must be prevented from buying it up or cutting it out. This requires that the neighborhood have regulatory power. Establishing a neighborhood economy means that the territory will generate as much wealth for its residents as is necessary for a good life in that territory. Note that we say the territory must generate wealth for its residents. It should not generate wealth primarily for outsiders, nor should its residents be totally dependent on resources outside the territory. The crux of the situation, again, is the improvement of territory by a territorial economy. It is only when the territory generates wealth principally for its residents that its people can be sure of local liberty.

Territorial economy requires that production for trade in the neighborhood is controlled by, and employs mainly, people living in the neighborhood. For this purpose, capital is the key factor, whether or not ownership of the means of production is in the hands of people living in the territory. Capital is needed—but it may be either real cash or credit. Ghetto neighborhoods have neither capital nor ownership, but this is not such a setback provided they obtain credit for the purchase and operation of productive technology. And as long as they meet their payments, we can call it ownership.

Now, how does a poor neighborhood obtain credit? Is there security in granting credit to black territory? Bankers say that default is most likely in black neighborhoods, where "they don't want to work." Credit for productive purchase is more likely to be extended to a neighborhood corporate organization. The difficulty is that even a strong organization has no collateral. Any urban property carries a high value; to obtain credit for production, therefore, it is necessary for the corporation both to have the power to tax its residents and to be able to dispose of its territory. This means the governmental power of eminent domain. Today, make no bones about it, when a neighborhood fails to pay its way, the government kicks the residents out and sells the land to private developers or other people. If a neighborhood corporation could do—or not do—the same for its territory, there would be no problem getting credit or mortgages, and less problem meeting payments. The typical conception of transferring capital to poor neighborhoods can now be viewed as within the purview of the neighborhood corporation which has gained the right of proprietorship to its territory—that is, the right to use it as the basis for credit, to mortgage a piece of it to keep it whole. In the real world this can be done in one of two ways: a private party can own it; or a government can do with it what it will, by virtue of political power and right. Why should the neighborhood undergo the ordeal of trying to own itself in the manner of a private entrepreneur when it can control itself as a government does? Allied with the issue of capital and production is the matter of regulatory power, needed by any government to maintain its economy. What we are dealing with is economic competition between neighborhoods: regulatory powers by which neighborhoods can wrest some productive and commercial independence from monopoly downtown ownership and control, and build independence through trade with other neighborhoods to prevent repeating the tendency toward the consolidation of wealth in one neighborhood. For example, it may be unrealistic for neighborhoods to mint their own currency, but it is reasonable for them to control prices, rents, licensing and banking.

The establishment of a territorial economy in neighborhoods is a crucial challenge to the present imperial economy of the city, which has been based on the commercial exploitation of the neighborhoods for the interests of downtown. Thus, the current glib discussion of economic development of poor neighborhoods in partnership with the private sector—which is, after all, downtown— and with the federal government obscures the real political struggle which the neighborhood corporations face for independent control of their local economy. The key to the development of a neighborhood economy is the political struggle for governing power.

TRANSFER VS. SEIZURE

This subject may be divided into two questions: first, by what means can the neighborhood gain local liberty from the central power; and, second, how can it maintain peace with other powers in order to build collective strength through alliance?

There are two strategies for gaining self-rule, either by seizure of public institutions and authority in the neighborhood or by the political transfer of authority from the central power brought about by political resistance and negotiations. We shall discuss later the method of transfer, a more appropriate strategy for the neighborhood unit. It is enough to say here that to the extent that established power refuses negotiated transfer, the neighborhoods will move toward direct seizure. The difficulty with direct seizure is that it invites the use of the military power of central authority—a force which is superior to that of any neighborhood. On the other hand, political resistance and negotiation are more suitable tactics for local power. The neighborhood must know at what times and over what issues it is propitious to demand self-rule, and it must know what will convince the central power to negotiate. Demonstrations, protests, boycotts, and other means of resisting central control and making demands for self-ruling authority should be employed in pressing this claim.

Both to advance local liberty and to defeat outside aggression, alliance with other neighborhoods and organizations is a major concern for neighborhood corporations. These are all instances of neighborhoods playing off one stronger power, either institutional or political, against another.

At another level, it is important for the neighborhood to build peaceful alliances with other neighborhoods of the city. For this purpose, it is important for local corporations which are leading the movement for self-rule to encourage the desire for local liberty in other territories of the city and to co-operate with them by sharing resources, such as money for organizing and personnel, as well as by employing shared strategies of collective action. The importance of joint strategy among equal territories cannot be overstated. The tendency of areas with local liberty is to become arrogant about their achievements and disdainful of other neighborhood organizations, but necessity dictates extensive alliances and co-operation. The neighborhood can very easily make the error of falling into alliance with stronger rather than equal powers.

LOCAL DEFENSE

The problem of local defense is different from that of gaining governing authority in the first place. Local defense deals with protecting local liberty from outside aggression. Although established power may transfer its authority, it will continually undermine such an agreement and endeavor to retract its transferred liberty. Thus, a continuing task of the neighborhood corporation is to defend its achieved authority and resources against outside power. In the event of attack, there are two basic means of this strategic defense. The first is outright military defense by local militias, such as the Blackstone Rangers and the Black Panthers. Because of the discrepancy in power between neighborhood force and police force, direct combat is of little value. Political resistance—for instance, nonco-operation, passive resistance, and subversion—is far more vital to local defense. Local authority may be lost if the community fails to prepare a defense. There are three means of prepared defense against outside power. The first, but least important, is military training (we have already discussed the superior military force of central power). At present, such military training is going on in the cities with the production and deployment of makeshift weapons. Yet in spite of the current excitement about it, history will show such military training to be a disaster for the purpose of defending local liberty. Much more important are political defenses of local rights. These entail bringing about the general political education of the locality, gaining the loyalty of the neighborhood citizens, and securing the local corporations against internal subversion. The aggression of central power is predominantly political and propagandistic, rather than military. Admittedly, we know about police assaults on black neighborhoods and universities, and this is unmistakably military. But because there is a limitation on permanently occupying and controlling neighborhoods, central power stresses subversion, propaganda, demoralization, intrigue, figurehead control, and other political means to mount offenses on local territory.

Often neglected, but the most important means of local defense, is changing the laws of central government to acknowledge *de facto* gains in local governing authority. The value of this legal revision for defense is that it formalizes general rights.

LEGISLATION

The chief object of neighborhood corporation is making just laws for its own community. The major categories of legislation are the health, education, welfare, and safety of the neighborhood. Programs dealing with these will bear the imprint of locality. For example, in education, an emphasis may be placed on training citizens for political deliberation in neighborhood corporate life. This is unlike the present character of national education, which does not train the young citizen to decide public matters, for he has no deliberative right.

There will be laws pertaining to the health of the neighborhood citizens. These will differ from present health laws, because their purpose will differ. Instead of making doctors rich, the communities will seek the health of their members and legislate programs that relate to the special health needs of the locality. Welfare programs will aim to be productive, rather than consigning the unemployed to uselessness.

Social legislation will originate in the deliberation of the community as it encounters actual events and needs. The drama of events shared and discussed by the people will be the foundation of legislation, not a scheme of priorities set by the outside central power. For example, an instance of violence and police brutality at a roller skating rink might be the occasion for corporate deliberation in which a great number of people would participate. They would express themselves on what they think the youth problem is, what the police problem is, and what the community should do about these problems. Ideas and feelings would be expressed in the deliberations as they could never be expressed when programs develop from an academic structuring of priorities. When a social program is decided on and begins, it will attract the same intense participation that its deliberation did, and it will represent the community's solution of the precipitating event. Participation is so poor in present-day centralized programs simply because they are developed on the basis of an abstractly deduced need precluding community involvement in its deduction. The foundation of such a "deduced" program rests in the theoretical thought of the outside analyst, not in the practical needs of the community.

In the final analysis, community legislation is the community's best defense. Even though preparedness to deal with outside aggression is necessary, no amount of defense training can protect the community from internal collapse due to ill-considered law, inept administration, or pronounced injustice.

6. *Local Territory and Political Environment*

Just as we have explored the purpose of neighborhood liberty, so too must we understand the physical area in which it may exist. The concept "neighborhood" has been unfashionable for so long that administrators and scholars, newly attracted to its use for urban development, have great difficulty in locating its territory. Some turn to techniques used in market research to determine its boundaries; others to sociometric and racial indices; still others to communication theory. Some look for social watersheds, others for indicators of local power. The sentimental style of sociology or the global orientation of politics obscures the territory of our neighborhoods.

Sociology has trained us to think of neighborhoods as units of good feeling in the madness of metropolitan life. But because the field and degree of good feeling expand or contract with time and circumstance, neighborhoods can seem as ephemeral as a disappearing act. When people love their city for some reason, experts think that the city is the neighborhood; yet, at other times, when people want desperately to escape to a suburb, they suppose that suburb in which they do not yet live is their neighborhood. Or when residents of a block develop a spirit of co-operation and form a clean-up club, it is surmised that the block is a neighborhood, even though it is only a block within a neighborhood, albeit one which is aiming to improve. When workers feel kindly toward their employer, experts even conclude the workplace is the neighborhood.

These views are in error. Neighborhoods exist simply as territorial facts whether they are loved or hated. Physical boundaries define neighborhoods—although some such divisions are more obvious than others. Another error made by "experts" is in wishful thinking about neighborhoods. The neighborhood is often confused with the size of the cause or cure of some particular problem. For example, if economic development is to solve poverty, the area which is subject to a new regional economic policy may be a region for capital investment, but it is not a neighborhood. For reasons of racial identity, some activists may postulate Harlem as the neighborhood of action against downtown, but, in fact, Harlem contains several neighborhoods. Units smaller than neighborhoods are sometimes selected for political organization, as when a block club is said to be the neighborhood for a nonprofit co-operative. But a block is not a neighborhood.

The most sensible way to locate the neighborhood is to ask people where it is, for people spend much time fixing its boundaries. Gangs mark its turf. Old people watch for its new faces. Children figure out safe routes between home and school. People walk their dogs through their neighborhood, but rarely beyond it. Above all, the neighborhood has a name: Hyde Park or Lake View in Chicago; Roxbury, Jamaica Plain, or Beacon Hill in Boston.

By asking people, we can find the boundaries of large neighborhoods and small ones, rich ones and poor ones, square and irregularly shaped ones. Whatever their size, shape, or style, they are the setting for many kinds of relationships. This diversity is joined into a common structure of action and character. So we often say that one neighborhood is dangerous or another neighborhood is fancy.

There are two principles which inform the commonly shared knowledge of neighborhood boundaries. Neighborhoods may be bounded by barriers that intensify local relationships. For example, new highways that radiate from downtown have sectioned off territories. From an airplane we can see how these freeways and beltways "moat" city areas into bounded territories. It is not unusual to find poor areas marked on two sides by eight-lane highways just beyond the center of the city. Urban renewal has also delineated neighborhoods. Land clearance and middle-income housing construction within the inner city have often reduced the size of poor areas and increased their population density. Proximity of middle-income construction has sharpened local identification within the older territory, at the same time that new neighborhoods are being settled within the adjacent renewed area.

Parks also delineate neighborhoods. In many cities, parks originated as common fields or private lands which lay between separate town or village settlements before they were annexed. Hyde Park, South Shore, Garfield Park, and Lawndale, in Chicago, are examples.

Physical boundaries are often reinforced by social relations. There is a tendency for prosperous neighborhoods to go to great lengths to establish physical defense barriers to outside traffic. The University of Chicago in Hyde Park, for instance, has attempted to seal itself off from the surrounding black neighborhoods. But this military tendency often invites more assault than it prevents. Natural boundaries are tolerable, but artificial perimeters are offensive.

Neighborhood territory has both boundary and center. This applies to social as well as to physical boundaries. Centers of local association are schools, settlement houses, community centers, supermarkets, and recreational facilities, and here one meets and becomes acquainted with people and comes to learn the limits of where they live. Beyond a certain point, people go to other centers.

Although there is no single place that everyone in the neighborhood goes to, there are places to which neighbors seem to have a greater right to or feeling of ease in than outsiders. This fact of "right of use," not the degree of actual use, is important in finding the center of neighborhoods. Several examples will make this clear. A child may go to a private school, but he does have a right to go to the local school rather than a public school across town. Even if he is bused, he feels less at ease in the distant neighborhood. Although the local settlement house or community center continually invites local residents to use its facilities, it does not extend the same invitation to people in another part of town. In many churches, parish ministers discourage people from other parts of town from forsaking their own parishes in favor of theirs.

In the historical development of the neighborhood, there has always been a primary political center, originally the meeting house or town hall of the neighborhood. When local governments became extinct, this sovereign center was lost. It is, however, significant that the political centers remain in the neigborhood; but now they are controlled by the outside power of downtown—examples are the alderman's office and the police station. In those cities which retain aldermanic election by ward districts, the alderman's office and ward boundaries are helpful signs of neighborhood boundaries, even if they have been gerrymandered to obscure historical identity. The wards of Chicago and Philadelphia still correspond somewhat to the cities, towns, and incorporated villages which they superseded. The last ward map of Pittsburgh before municipal reform and the city-wide election of the council began is an excellent political portrait of present-day neighborhoods, which were annexed boroughs, cities, and villages. Although the meeting house for the town assembly is gone, the alderman maintains a list and records of neighborhood residents, just as a town clerk formerly did. And with as little uncertainty as the town clerk, he knows who is a resident of the neighborhood and who is not.

The maintenance of public schools was a principal activity of the town. Admission was limited to the town children, just as it is today except when there is busing; children must attend schools within their neighborhood boundaries. The settlement house replaced the old town poorhouse, as voluntary charity replaced the old poor tax. Parks replace the old town commons and offer many of the same public uses, such as sports and entertainment, drawing together the local residents, even if open markets and training fields are things of the past. Local libraries serve areas that correspond to neighborhoods.

From these centers of public activity we can survey the boundaries of neighborhood association. We will see that although neighborhoods are generally small, they vary in size. Their general population range within cities is from 2,500 to 75,000 residents. Their areas generally range from one-half square mile to six square miles. Yet neighborhood size does not vary with the total population and land area of a city. The territorial extent of neighborhoods was already fixed when they lost independence. Thus, when Morrisania was annexed to the Bronx, it contained fourteen incorporated villages which correspond to present-day neighborhoods. Neighborhoods of Brooklyn —for instance, Flatbush, Bushwick, Coney Island, New Utrecht, and Williamsburg—are about the same size as when they were annexed by downtown Brooklyn.

Within the population and area range of neighborhoods, the political environment of the city affects the strategy of local organization for self-rule.

MUNICIPAL GOVERNMENT

Cities in which municipal councils are elected at large are more favorable to neighborhood corporations in poor areas than are cities where councils are elected by ward districts. Because at-large councils are elected by the middle-class majority of the city, they concentrate political organizations and public services in middle-class areas.

As a result, there are no established political party organizations to meet local needs in poor areas. Instead, a political vacuum awaits new authority. The territorially defined neighborhood corporation can fill this vacuum without immediately threatening the political prerogatives of the city council. In such cities—for instance, Boston, Pittsburgh, Detroit, and San Francisco—the neighborhood corporation may not encounter initial political opposition, as it would where the city council is elected by ward districts, as in Chicago.

Although the council elected at large will ignore the neighborhood development, the mayor of such a city may see the advantage of co-operating with the corporately organized voters of the neighborhood community. By relating positively to the poor through their neighborhood corporation, he can gain a maximum return of good will for his support of their corporate demands to share authority over social services and resources. He will also find the neighborhood corporation a more stable structure for negotiations with localities than the plethora of special interest and ad hoc protest organizations.

BUREAUCRACY

A vital prerogative for self-governing neighborhoods is the authority to administer local programs of social and community service, and this must be wrested from the bureaucracy of city government. In cities where the council is elected at large, there is little political inducement to serve poor areas. The argument to transfer authority to the neighborhood corporation can proceed without much challenge to the bureaucracy, which does little in the territory. Where, however, the bureaucracy is entrenched in poor areas, as it is in Chicago, the claim for local authority will initially be resisted by the city administration. The amount of bureaucratic resistance will be an indicator of the extent of professional organization and resources of the social administration of the city. Where these are large, opposition will be great, and bureaucrats will forcefully oppose neighborhood claims for independent authority. Where the bureaucracy is politically weak, prospects for local control are more favorable. In New York City, an example of the strength of bureaucratic opposition was the resistance of the teachers' union to school decentralization. It must be anticipated that a bureaucracy will oppose neighborhood control with great resources of money and heavy ideological attack, and will label the corporation a menace to democracy, efficiency, and quality. Bureaucratic opposition, and its implicit threat of a public employees' strike if a transfer proceeds, can exert great force and prevent political interests from supporting a transfer of authority to neighborhood corporations. Even where the social service bureaucracy is neither politically strong nor self-conscious, it will resist giving neighborhoods authority over social service administration. Such a confrontation must, however, be fought with a political strategy of threats of equivalent disorder and protest. Great care must be exercised in reaching a negotiated settlement.

In a city environment, there are also social differences in neighborhoods which affect the strategy for organizing for self-rule, such as social class, existing resources, and political demand.

Class

There is more pressure for incorporation and self-governing authority in poor than in well-to-do neighborhoods. This does not mean that the value of neighborhood corporation is exclusive to the poor, but that prospects for its development are presently more favorable in poor areas. Although the middle class enjoys prosperity through privilege, the poor need neighborhood government to secure the liberty to achieve prosperity.

Four factors favor corporate development in poor neighborhoods. Because of unemployment, many residents of poor neighborhoods spend more time within their areas than do residents of wealthier neighborhoods. Further, the employment pattern in poor neighborhoods corresponds to that of seasonal or unskilled workers, and this has the same effect as unemployment in reinforcing neighborhood rather than job location as the strongest unit of familiar public relationship.

In addition to spending more time in the neighborhoods, poor residents spend more time outdoors, because they usually have numerous children and live in congested housing conditions. This means more intensive public gathering on sidewalks, at churches, and in stores in the neighborhood. With intense public life comes a greater development of co-operation in order to make street life tolerable.

Although most people commit what is considered a crime at some time, the poor are punished more often because they lack the knowledge of how to protect themselves, the shield of social status, and the resources to

extricate themselves. The intense penalization they encounter makes them view statutory law as illegitimate and
local custom as legitimate. The desire of the urban poor
to codify the force of custom bears the strongest potential
for development of the self-governing legal structure of
the neighborhood corporation. The charter and by-laws
of neighborhood corporations, developed by the people of
poor neighborhoods, will give greater force to the form of
their organization.

In years past, intense organizing has occurred in poor
areas. Ad hoc organizations dealing with school desegrega-
tion, welfare rights, housing, job discrimination, etc., have
initiated a political dialogue in poor areas, and this is a
significant foundation for the deliberative process of the
assembly-based neighborhood corporation. The important
aspect of this dialogue is that it has been concerned with
local public issues, not national interpretations of local
problems. Furthermore, discussion has been public, taking
the forms of mass meetings, protest demonstrations, and
community organizing. In middle-class neighborhoods, on
the other hand, issues are discussed in small, private
groups and committees. In dealing with housing, organizational activity in white neighborhoods has taken the form
of preventing Negroes from purchasing houses or schools
from desegregating, and such activities have been con-
ducted secretly. Arrangements are made with real estate
agents behind closed doors. Individual owners are pressured not to sell or rent to Negroes. This is not the kind of
organizational practice that is in keeping with the style
of public deliberation of the neighborhood corporation.

Ultimately, the area in which it is most practical to
transfer authorities to neighborhoods is that which con-

cerns social and community services. Such services are obviously less vital to the well-to-do than to the poor, who cannot afford to pay privately for baby-sitters, job training, education, health services, and youth recreation. Accordingly, the poor neighborhoods are more inclined to organize for local control of such services.

Existing Resources

Another aspect which is favorable to local rule is the presence of community services—for instance, community centers, settlement houses, and antipoverty centers. Where these exist, community services are already structured and administered, even if they are controlled by outside powers. The actual benefits and drawbacks of the community services are known to people, and the potential of their resources under self-governing authority is understood, if not expressed. Where such services do not exist, the possible benefits of placing them under local control are not understood. Where private agencies of community service do exist, it is easier for their control to be transferred to the neighborhood than for the neighborhood to gather the original resources.

Political Demand

Perhaps the most important criterion for local control is whether the people of the neighborhood claim the authority to govern local affairs. This elusive element of claim is a reflection of the spirit of independence within the community. A claim of political authority emanates from lengthy community consideration of the many public issues that can cause people distress, until they realize that local problems are caused by bad *laws,* and can be solved only when the community is empowered to make its own laws.

This claim may be expressed heatedly or in a cool manner. A cool-tempered approach sets the scene for a more effective struggle, because the central power is more likely to transfer authority to those who make a temperate claim than to those who harshly state demands, since it is easier to give gifts than to do justice. Furthermore, when authority is given, that transfer constitutes a gift. Such a transaction made on the basis of good sense and good will augurs well for the continuing relationship of giver and receiver.

7. *The Transfer of Authority*

The difficulty of discussing the transfer of authority from the central power to the neighborhood community is that there are two audiences to address and two sets of arguments to make. People must be persuaded to claim political authority for their localities, and central power must be persuaded to give it away.

The people today are angry, fearful and contemptuous of the government, and both the rhetoric and the physical expression of rebellion are becoming increasingly violent. This situation may lead to forceful repression of dissent and rebellion by the central government; it may die out for internal reasons (although this is the least likely possibility), or it may result in revolution.

We are conditioned to think of revolution as *national* change, whether as a final element in a nationalist revolution or an intermediate element in the vanguard of in-

ternational revolution—but essentially as a change in the
national structures of power. A new nationalism to replace
the old! A just nationalism, even a participatory nationalism! Some seek a black nationalism, but again, it is the
nation reborn.

But the democratic aim of local liberty does not depend
on a change in the national power structure. *Local* control
must be the preliminary fact and remain the final object
of political revolution.

The attainment of this objective requires that people
demand it. To do so, we must regain an understanding of
the sufficiency of locality if political liberty is ever to be
reinstituted. Too, we must develop a capacity for governing after years of being ruled.

The only way to surmount these difficulties is through
political education based on the practice of local control.
While people seethe with revolutionary emotions, they
do not easily comprehend the necessity for political liberty,
and for this reason tend to respond to ideology—e.g.,
"black power," or "workers' control." They do, however,
have specific interests—better schools, or changes in the
welfare laws, for example—because they see these things
as improving their condition. Once they move on these
matters and begin to gain some degree of local authority,
they begin to see the necessity of actually controlling the
schools, or their local economies, etc. By observing the
utility of control in other communities and practicing it
in their own, they learn what liberty is and realize the
political sufficiency of the local community.

Once the demand for local government is articulated,
the problem becomes one of getting those who have con-

trol to give it to the community. And every instance of peaceful transfer of authority to the community increases the popular understanding of the revolutionary object of local control.

The second difficulty in transfer is self-evident: it is that official power is not inclined to give away its authority.

There is nothing more terrifying to a bureaucrat than the prospect of losing control over the lives of his clients. To lose these small opportunities for tyranny means the loss of the personal power that our paternalistic system gives bureaucrats as a fringe benefit and calls moral obligation. Having no political liberty themselves, administrators cannot understand the claim of local liberty—let alone appreciate it. Their little control over a few lives blinds them to their own political oppression in a life of privilege without liberty.

Furthermore, those currently in control are made to feel secure in their positions by the police power at their disposal. In a political climate where riots are a constant threat, they interpret all local claim as a violation of law and order, to enable intervention of the police.

Yet, for two reasons, their sense of security may be false, or at least weakening. In the first place, in highly volatile but not yet riotous situations, officials are frequently reluctant to send in police for fear of worsening the disorder, and may even be compelled to accede, at least temporarily, to the demands of the people. In the second place, the police have their own political interests, which may profit by their violence upon the community, not necessarily to the support of the threatened sector of bureaucracy.

Thus we arrive at an understanding of the official's point

of view, and can see that only one factor really compels transfer of authority: that is, sheer utility. A union of welfare workers which prefers to retain control over its clients may give up some of that control rather than lose its physical property or subject its members to assault. Mayor Lindsay argued from the standpoint of sheer practicality when he persuaded New York City's School Board to give three communities control over their own schools.

There is another factor, although potentially less convincing, which encourages officials to transfer a part of their authority to the people. Many bureaucrats are dissatisfied with the system as it exists, and political education can exploit their discontent to some degree. Although such education may be effective only to the point of getting them to grant rather limited jurisdictions to neighborhood organizations, such a step is progress. It also has the crucial benefit of giving officials, too, practice in liberty. And only through practice, for those in power as well as for those seeking it, can men come to feel no longer threatened by revolution, but freed.

At this point the question of violent seizure of control may legitimately be raised. Transfer, we have seen, is not accomplished overnight; it requires political understanding and the employment of persuasion and tact on both sides. For this reason we may ask, "Why wait? Why not simply take over—forcefully—the institutions of authority?"

The answer is obvious: such a maneuver would bring immediate military force on a large scale against the community, which it lacks the power to combat. Therefore, except in a few very specifically defined situations, the neighborhood organization must negotiate for transfer. Violence completely changes the complexion of events. A convincing argument may be made that violence used to gain local political objectives can never succeed except for limited periods; to sustain success it must be nationally reinforced.

One exception to this general rule may be cited. Direct seizure, without the capability to maintain it militarily, may be possible when the community already has *de facto* control of an institution. But even in this case, that *de facto* authority will usually have been gained by means of negotiation and transfer.

8. The Organization of Neighborhood Politics

We must now examine the ways in which the neighborhood can maintain and build the authority transferred from central government and build the capability for real government. As we have discussed, location, population, and social organization affect the power of the neighborhood corporation. Whether power is secured depends on whether the form of community rule makes the most of these conditions.

Political power has two components: prudent decision and forceful action. The neighborhood corporation has the task of arranging authority among the people so that their decisions form practical solutions to common problems, and their actions are effective. In this way, neighborhood corporation may evolve into neighborhood government.

In the United States, we have been told so often that our government is "democratic" that we have failed to realize that it is only representative. Once we elect our representatives, our voice in day-to-day political decision is lost: that power in America rests ultimately with officials. In a practically constituted neighborhood government, on the other hand, although it may be representative to a great extent, lawmaking power remains in the *demos*—the people. This is imperative because a democracy (one man, one vote) is the only arrangement that can bring the total power of a community into its political organization. Direct democracy at this level is also practical, although at a larger level it is not. Assembly is already a social institution; the problem is only to secure political authority for it.

This does not mean that a government based on direct democracy contains no divisions or stratifications of power. We can conveniently examine its form on two levels, the legislative and the executive.

LEGISLATIVE POWER

Several institutions in which people already assemble exist in any neighborhood. Even before they form neighborhood corporations, people go to church, have mass meetings, and belong to neighborhood clubs. On the basis of these experiences, people are prepared to assemble to make laws. Columbus' ECCO (discussed in detail in Chapter 4) illustrates one way deliberative citizenship can operate.

The corporation meets annually by law to elect the executive council and to conduct legislative business, and for these meetings 10 per cent of the membership constitutes a quorum. It can also meet on the call of fifty members or by decision of any of its four neighborhood

districts. Only the assembly has the authority to elect offi-
cers, to remove them for cause, to approve or terminate
any corporate programs, to amend the by-laws of the corporation, to investigate neighborhood problems, and to
initiate programs to meet the community's needs.

An issue always raised by advocates of representative
government is the level of attendance at assembly meetings. In ECCO, attendance generally runs between 10
and 25 per cent of the membership. Critics claim 10
per cent is not sufficiently representative of the people
for legislative purposes. They argue that representative
democracy is more broadly based. But this is a specious
argument, amounting to little more than a numbers game.
We frequently find, particularly in off-election years, that
representatives are elected by only as many—if not fewer
—voters as convene in assembly for direct decision. In
many election districts, fewer than 25 per cent of
eligible voters go to the polls. If it is argued that it is
at least possible for a representative to win 70 per
cent of the votes in his district, it can be said that it is
equally possible for the same percentage of citizens to attend the democratic assembly. When there are political
crises, assembly attendance rises.

A more fundamental argument is that a small quorum of
members is quite sufficient to bring all political positions of
concern and interest to the forum for deliberation. Even a
10 per cent quorum usually encompasses the widest existing range on political opinion and emotion. (Representative government, after all, permits a spectrum of only two
candidates, running on two or three issues at best, and on
mere personality at worst, every few years.)

Popular deliberation in the ECCO area also takes place through the four districts into which the community is divided. Although these districts are independent organizations, they function as political clubs of the neighborhood corporation. Each club elects four members of the executive council annually; the general assembly elects the remaining fourteen at large. These clubs represent distinct local interests and political attitudes, and through them the deliberation of the membership takes place on a continuing basis. Program development is often initiated by the clubs, for it is within their small districts that dramatic events often occur.

Clubs also represent the sectional interests of the localities within the neighborhood. Because the clubs existed before incorporation, they became factions in the assembly, but they are not political parties.

Finally, a vital function performed by the neighborhood clubs is the development of political leadership. Their independent meetings offer opportunities for formation of new popular leaders, who move into the assembly with district support and eventually achieve official positions on the council or executive staff. It is within the clubs that new leaders get political training and ideas. Since their statements in the assembly are sustained by club support, their rhetoric becomes more confident. An assembly without internal political groups and strategies would have no motion or direction.

Another dimension of deliberation, although relatively minor initially, is the committee structure of the council. Only at a later stage of ECCO's development, when legislation becomes more complex, is it likely that committees will assume major importance. The committees are chaired by council members, but their meetings are open to any member of the corporation. Through an open committee structure, therefore, community participation in the government is further reinforced.

The democracy of the assembly, clubs, and open committees is of crucial importance because it brings the most complete collective agreement to combat political opposition from central power. If a man shares in the deliberative authority of public life, he will commit his own power to defend the corporate body, even though he may be in the minority on many decisions. He will defend the corporation for the sake of his own deliberative right, but he is not apt to defend it if all decision is left to one executive or to an elected council.

Another reason for legislation by assembly is that it will serve the common interest, not special interests. Lawmaking by an assembly of citizens will favor the many rather than the few, simply because wealth and special interest have a smaller voice in the public assembly than in elected councils.

EXECUTIVE POWER

The equality of assembly is a necessary principle for neighborhood power, but it is not sufficient for effective government. The people enact legislation, but the assembly is too unwieldy a structure to administer it. In a neighborhood corporation, executive power must be delegated —but to an elected council rather than a single executive director or a paid staff.

This may be difficult to understand, because we generally identify executive power with a single official—for instance, the President—but it is important for two reasons.

When executive power is concentrated in a single person, its main consequence is to encourage personal ambition. If our goal is a self-contained government, be it a neighborhood corporation or a state, which uses its power for internal growth and improvement and exists in cooperative relation to other units, then personal ambition must be checked.

The tendency of those who hold elective office is to want to retain their positions, for reasons of either power or honor. This is also true of executive office even when the people make law in the assembly. When only one man is elected, his desire for re-election will direct the use of the entire executive power to that end, and a personal style of office-holding, not effective implementation of the laws, will be favored. When executive office is divided among several people, administrative resources cannot be monopolized by the political ambition of one, and law, not office, will be served.

Only two principles can contain the natural tendency of unified executive power to become tyrannical through manipulation of administration: first, the equality of the people themselves and their power to make law; and second, the division of executive power in an elected council.

Thus, we see the importance of the elected council as the source of executive power and administration. The council, elected by the assembly, will reflect the variety of forces in the assembly's laws and give operational power to such differences as are reflected in the law.

A final importance of the executive council is that it gives the distinction of public office to political leadership. The desire for honor is a natural fact of political life, and the corporation must provide honorable offices to fulfill this desire. It is also the case that the moral character honored by the people in election will reflect the very virtues that can secure a just administration of the laws.

9. *Localism, Not Separatism*

The movement for neighborhood government through local control does not aim for complete separation of localities from the state, but for their self-government and representation within it. Through this process, which leads to a federated city, the people will regain the deliberative capacity of citizenship in their local assembly, and the state will regain popular support.

Obstacles to local rule arise not only in the transference of authority, but also in the tendency toward separatism within the movement for local control.

There are many people of good will in American society who think that black communities should sever all relations with white society. Neighborhood government challenges this separatism, and instead seeks the inclusion of localities, black and white, into the general government.

There are two sources of separatist tendencies in the

movement for local control. One emerges from a conception of self-interest among blacks—"black power"—the
other from perilous compassion among whites. For blacks,
the separatist tendency is the outgrowth of a decade of
civil rights organization and their strategy of creating
black organizations parallel to established institutions,
such as the Mississippi Freedom Democratic Party, and
freedom schools, which were organized to encourage collective action and define black identity. In Mississippi,
SNCC was able to bring black people together in political
action on the basis of such parallel programs. They also
served as simulations of social and political institutions and
gave people a chance to experience what politics is, and
how humanistic values would require different social institutions. In addition, these programs were of strategic
use, for they probed to find whether established government could accept these institutions of the people by
granting them legal and political authority. If society
could accommodate both dimensions of parallel organizations—their public power and the humaneness of their
new social arrangements—social change could advance
peacefully with the sanction of state authority.

This test of peaceful incorporation of independent institutions into society was the greatest significance of parallel
organizations. As the embodiment of a theory of peaceful
revolution, they were implicitly disposed toward negotiation and change within the context of transferred authority.
Of course, negotiation had limits. Parallel organizations
could not bargain away their own control of these new
institutions entirely, even if the state agreed for a moment
to run the specific program advanced. Nor could the state

transfer its entire authority over public institutions to popular control. Yet within these limits, parallel organizations found room for agreement and change. The direction of this approach was not separatist, but integrationist. The black community was already separated. It was excluded from power and was seeking to come into society with the power of independent institutional authority. Yet, in emphasizing parallel organization, rather than trying to gain control of existing institutions, it erred, for when established power refused to grant them authority, the resultant frustration and bitterness forced them toward separatism.

For the state cannot transfer a public authority, like education, to a political group which does not have legal control of the territory that institution serves. That is the essence of private power in America. Institutional authority goes with territorial control, and one power cannot hold the institution if another power holds the territory.

As a result of the emphasis on institutional, rather than territorial, authority and representation, the course of parallel organization dwelt too heavily on cultural identity but did not achieve institutional authority for its expression. The political frustration which ensued stretched cultural differences to the point of political separation. For although culture is intrinsically exclusive, territorial authority is not. A stress on local territorial authority and representation at the state level would have better served the interests of black political power than the parallelism which led only to a powerless culture.

The source of separatism in white liberalism is its rejection of political liberty—right to govern—in favor of civil rights or liberties—personal freedom from government. This emphasis diverges from the black strategy to gain power to govern.

Whites abandoned the right to govern for the privilege of economic pursuits. Because blacks were cut out of the economy early in the game, their only option is to seek political control to legislate themselves back in.

Neighborhood government moves toward territorial public power as the basis of creating new social institutions. Furthermore, having government authority is more fundamental to changing social conditions than having a vital economic role.

The strategy of white liberal politics is the opposite; it aims to increase its political power through its economic role.

The black radical faces an essentially different political problem from the white. If we view in juxtaposition the cultural separatism of the black movement and the white fixation on central economic power, we see a powerful tendency to exclude the black from the national order. It is important to understand that black separatist polemics are often intended as strategic approaches to gain political authority through local control.

Because of the national tendencies in the white community which reinforce separatism, black politics must be particularly careful to make links from neighborhood government to higher levels of power. The guiding principle must be to build territorial structures of local control, based on transferred power and local representation in the state, so that the neighborhood becomes a constitutional unit of government.

This requires both state presence in the locality and local

representation in the state. Only as the state maintains its presence of authority in neighborhood government will neighborhood government gain and retain public power and resources from the state. The moment the state entirely departs from black neighborhoods, the authority of neighborhood government will collapse into warfare against an outside power.

By gaining legal authority, the neighborhood government participates in the constituted power of the state. This has no value for purposes of separatism. It is not only endangered by such a policy; it is also the best protection against it.

10. The Radical Politics of Local Control

There is an obsession in the land with devising new social programs as solutions to riots, racism, poverty, and the hundred or so other terms of the present unrest and disorder. There are antipoverty programs, model cities programs, and a host of legislated contrivances. The search for the key program to get at the root of our troubles continues with unabated energy. Yet all share a common failing: they are all programs legislated by the central government—whether federal, state, or municipal—and controlled by outside central power.

Even those who proclaim themselves sympathetic to "neighborhood power" think of neighborhood corporation as little more than an administrative mechanism for carrying out centrally devised programs—the enduring mark of liberal reform.

Reason, though suffused with passion, can still enable us

to understand the disorders of society and their political solutions. But there the power of reason is halted. We approve social progress but we refuse to see that what is necessary for change will affect our privileged position. We purport to be revolutionary, while seeking to stand outside a changing world on some stable ground.

So much for the liberals and the old bore-from-within theory. A new left politics is challenging the liberal view, and risking the unstable ground of direct confrontation with the government. The only difficulty with this strategy is that it aims only to gain control of the national government.

True radicalism issues from a practical view of man's political nature, rather than a theoretical view of the state. Its object is to shape the state to fit the present purpose of popular struggle—local rule—not to reshape man to fit a theoretical state. For the left to engage in politics of liberty requires that it free itself of the modern heritage of revolution and address the principles of local control.

CLASS OR COMMUNITY

Although the concept of community has received polemical and theoretical attention from the left, its understanding of community remains confused with Marxist notions of class struggle. It is difficult for them, however young and bold, to free themselves from the theoretical tradition that underpinned a century of revolution. Youth identifies with examples of successful action—Chinese and Cuban revolutions. They accept the theoretical reasoning behind those struggles, for it is only that theory which promises success to their own action. Yet, so often the theoretical reason for revolution postdates its action and success. The Chinese, even today, endeavor to understand the mysteries of their own revolution. And the reason, or theory, which dissolves their wonder at events becomes gospel in other parts of the world that hope for successful rebellion.

In one breath, the left speaks of community power; in another, of the political union of all the poor. The latter appeal carries the residual notion of class, but certain problems fragment its meaning and expression. The poor, white and black, which they would like to see unified, are largely unemployed or marginally employed. They are the impoverished thirty million in the United States. Unlike the unemployed or impoverished industrial workers during the last century, these millions have no essential relation to the production of wealth in the society. They are an extruded class. Or rather, not a class at all, but more an estate bound to land—urban or rural—than to production.

The basis of class struggle is the essential relation of each class to the production of wealth. Since wealth could not accrue without the triangle of ownership, labor, and consumption, the economic competition of classes was the dynamic nexus of political change.

In our age of increasing technology and the reduction of labor, the thirty million poor are not a class in this traditional sense. They are outside the economic process. They neither own, work, nor consume to any significant degree. Yet they are politically acting—a fact that no theory of class struggle can explain.

To dismiss their economic power is one thing, but to dismiss their political power and the present force of their collective strength is another thing entirely. They are moving to control their own estate not on the basis of their economic power, but rather to control their land through community power.

Community power, as understood by the leftists, attempts to correct these difficulties of defective class organization. They form unions of the poor as if mere organization could qualify them for the class struggle. The economy does not respond to their demands, because, however organized, they are not an economic class.

Aside from the economic principle of political organization, there is a local principle—older and more basic than class. Although the poor today play no essential role in the national system of production, they are essential to the territorial organization of the state. An alienated population with its own impregnable locality is an ultimate danger to the nation.

We start with certain facts. The urban poor, predominantly black, are a growing percentage of our urban population and constitute a local society within an established social order. They occupy the central areas of all the major cities. Their rioting endangers the economy, with no loss to them. This power even federal troops have the greatest difficulty crushing.

Territoriality is the great political asset of the black urban poor. But territoriality is not only an efficient political tactic: it is a natural impulse of threatened people. Thus, reason and nature move the poor toward territorial control as a lever of political change for greater justice.

From authority over and self-government of local territory, political power will grow and exchange its territorial loyalty and support of the state for resources useful for internal development and economy.

Recognizing this vital principle of territorial control by which the poor can act politically, we see that its method differs from that of class organization. Territorial control is aided not by a union of all the poor, but by the political organization of particular localities. Because the loyalty of each local territory is vital to the state, the movement for local control advances the entire estate.

NATIONALISM OR LOCALISM

The fundamental character of modern revolution has been local insurrection against the central power of the state. This was true in the American Revolution, where the towns rebelled against provincial government; of the communes in the French Revolution, and of the self-ruling Soviets during the Russian Revolution. It is only afterwards, through the efforts of a party such as the Federalists, Girondists, or Bolsheviks, that the revolution is centralized and local democracy is crushed by nationalism. In America, the instrument of central control was the federal Constitution, which recognized the sovereignty of state governments to annex towns and their governments. In Russia, the soviets were abolished by party centralism.

We are compelled by a fact of democratic revolution: it is a local event; and democracy is achieved only through local control. The central dilemma of revolution is how the democracy of local control can withstand the nationalist re-establishment of central power.

The same tendency is implicit in the leftist call for participatory democracy under a new structure of national power. A radical change in the structure of national power is not a revolution, but its subversion.

The object of revolution is political liberty, which is established by local insurrection and control. Its success rests in preserving local liberty. To the extent that the left promotes the concept of social equality, it is wedded to nationalism, not to democratic revolution. As a result, it organizes not for revolution, which abolishes national power, but for a *coup d'état*.

In addition to their desire to domestically redistribute wealth, the left's attachment to national power stems from their preoccupation with foreign policy. They want equality on a global scale—world revolution. But since revolution is a fact of *local* liberty, their goal amounts only to imperialism.

The radical task which the left must undertake if it is to assist democratic revolution is to challenge the very concept of nationalism and central control. To be radical, intellectual and physical force must accord with the original phenomena of revolution—local insurrection and local control—within which structure democracy can flourish. The left must develop and articulate a theory of local sovereignty. Their term "community power" has potential for such development, but only if "community" is understood as simply the method of gaining and preserving local democratic control.

LIBERTY OR SOCIAL CHANGE

Another confusion which the left must clarify in order to come to terms with democratic revolution is the conflict between social equality and political liberty. With a new arrangement of national power based on participatory democracy, they say, social institutions can be reorganized to meet real human needs instead of artificially contrived ones.

The difficulty with this formula is that it is merely an argument for their central control of revolution, not the purpose of political revolution. That purpose is never social change, but political liberty, which requires local self-rule.

In addition to the social inequities of millions in this nation, there is a worse poverty, shared by the poor and the affluent. It is the impoverishment of political life, which results from the growth of central administration. As administration advances its control, the possibilities for legitimate political activity by the people diminish. The primary aspect of political liberty is local deliberation, and administration always contends against the people for the monopoly of deliberative control.

Radical politics must comprehend the political movement of people toward local sovereignty. This, not national social equalization, is the political principle of revolutionary impulse today. Radical politics must understand that social equality is not the object of political revolution, but its opposing force. The left must decide whether it wants social change or political revolution; benign administration or political life; social engineering or political freedom; participatory democracy or local control. If it chooses the latter, radical politics will find that the middle class, as well as the poor, have a personal stake in revolution. This conception of revolution will free radical politics of its compassionate malaise.

Epilogue

A NEW CONSTITUTION

We are a nation of cities. That is where the people live and the wealth is centered. That our attention has been turned to world power and global conquest, and our wealth siphoned by national power for that purpose, does not alter this fact. Nor are we any less an urban nation because our cities are the domain of downtown commercial power, or because the federal Constitution fails to acknowledge that these empires exist. The result of these facts is that our cities are impoverished economically and oppressed politically. It is from this circumstance that the movement for local control arises in rebellions across the land. Not until the cities can use a greater part of their wealth and have better governments can we expect any domestic peace. Neither half of this whole will satisfy the situation. To apply more resources to the ruling oligarchies of our cities will only drive us further toward a police state, and to accept the authority of the neighborhoods to control their own public life without granting them fair resources to do so is equally dangerous.

The struggle of local control to achieve neighborhood government leads us to the fundamental necessity of a new political constitution of our cities to return rule and wealth to its communities.

What we face today is a constitutional crisis. This does not mean a failure only of the federal Constitution, which grants power to the states in order to bind them into a nation, but also that the people of our cities have no legitimate political constitution to bind their neighborhoods in peace.

All cities are chartered by state governments, and new charters must be approved by them. At present, hundreds of cities are writing new charters. This has gone on for a long time and usually results from the need of city governments for greater powers to control the neighborhoods. These charters have always been written from the center, and the people are urged to approve them.

Such charters are not political constitutions for the cities, but rather distributions of control of them between the political machines of downtown and the state government. Whatever the new protestations by the rulers of our cities for home rule, or by our state governments to clean up city administrations, they do not alter this division of spoils, which results when people do not have the sovereignty to constitute themselves. Even today, charter commissions are trying to accommodate the local control movement by promising a neighborhood role in their new designs. But this will not do.

The object of neighborhood government requires that

the communities of our cities confront these charter commissions. They must use this confrontation as the basis for convening local assemblies in the neighborhood to deliberate about the rights and resources they need to govern their own communities. From there, the neighborhoods can ally themselves to devise city constitutions that distribute power among the neighborhoods and federate that power in a common city government.

Obviously, there will be a fight between the neighborhoods and the special interests in the city who will oppose it. But it is by no means clear today that these groups have the power to prevent a popular ratification.

The greater political struggle lies in the confrontation between a popularly supported constitution and the state government. What the federal government would do in this struggle, when its aid is called upon by both the people and the state government, remains to be seen, for it has its own national interests. It may, as it has many times in the past, support the state government and its interests and move against the people. The action it takes will depend upon its power at the time.

Today, national power is being shaken on two fronts. On the one hand, its international commitments have alienated the people, and on the other, people are rebelling for local control. In the face of these considerations, federal power may not side with the state governments, but instead support the cities.

In the final analysis, the most salutary fact in favor of new governments for our cities is that they are too vast to be dominated and must have their own sovereignty. And the basis of that sovereignty must be the federation of its local territories, the neighborhoods.

Index

Alinsky, Saul, 27; theory of local organization, 27-30

Allegheny, Pennsylvania, annexation of surrounding towns by, 20-21; incorporated by Pittsburgh, 1905, 5, 20, 21; territory and population of, 17

American Revolution, local character of, 99; political parties preceding, 24

Annexation, argument for, 7-8; as factor of commercial growth, 21; as factor of urban growth, 19-20; as factor in population growth, 21-22; effects of, 5-6, 10, 16; opposition to, 28; purpose of, 15-19

Bedford-Stuyvesant Community Corporation, 36, 40

Black capitalism, as approach to community organization, 36-7

Black nationalism, as approach to community organization, 33-4

Black Panthers, 58

Blackstone Rangers (Chicago), 30, 58

Bolsheviks, in Russian Revolution, 99

Boston, Massachusetts, and annexation of Roxbury, 4, 10; and annexation of Dorchester Neck, 15, 17; and annexation of Dorchester, Charleston, Roxbury, 24; form of municipal government, 25, 69; petitioned by Dorchester Neck for separation, 18; town meeting government in, 23

Bronx, New York, annexed by New York City, 20; annexation of Morrisania, 3, 68

Brooklyn, New York, annexed by New York City, 20, 21; annexation of Bushwick, Flatbush, 5, 68; annexation of Coney Island, New Utrecht, Williamsburg, 68; population growth of, 21-2, 68

Browne, Robert S., 33

BUILD (Buffalo, New York), 27

Bushwick, New York, annexed by Brooklyn, 5, 20, 68